I0569253

HASHEM GAVE US LIGHT — LET'S USE IT!

How are you feeling this season?
Have you slowed down a little — wrapped yourself in a cozy sweater,
put on fuzzy socks and poured yourself a cup of hot tea?
Have you taken the time to care for your mind, body and soul?
I know you're busy, but have you paused to think about
what truly brings you joy, meaning, and keeps your inner spark alive?

Are you smiling — or maybe giving me that half-sarcastic,
half-knowing smile right now?

That's good. Our sages teach that
"the light on a person's face comes from the joy in their heart."

This season, the world glitters and bustles with celebrations that often replace
meaning with materialism — moments that shine on the surface but fade quickly.
Amid all that noise and sparkle, we are gifted something eternal: the holiness
of Shabbat and the pure light of Chanukah...or Hanukkah. :)

Shabbat gathers us every single week, reminding us that connection and
meaning aren't limited to one day a year — they're part of our divine rhythm,
a light that never fades.

And then comes Chanukah — our festival of light in the heart of winter.
Eight special nights to reconnect, to bring holiness into our homes,
to celebrate miracles, resilience, and truth — to let the *Emet,*
the pure divine truth, stand out in the darkness of confusion
that surrounds the world.

I am overjoyed and grateful for this beautiful global collection of
Jewish women's voices — made for you. Inside this edition, you'll find stories,
wisdom, tips, and creativity that speak to every generation of Jewish women.
If you see a contact under an article you enjoyed, please reach out,
connect and share the goodness.

I hope this edition brings you warmth, comfort and light — and that your
Chanukah will be beautiful and meaningful, wherever you are and whatever
you're going through.

It's time to celebrate being Jewish even more — proudly, joyfully, and together.
Happy Winter & Chanukah Sameach!

Naomi Journo &
The Team

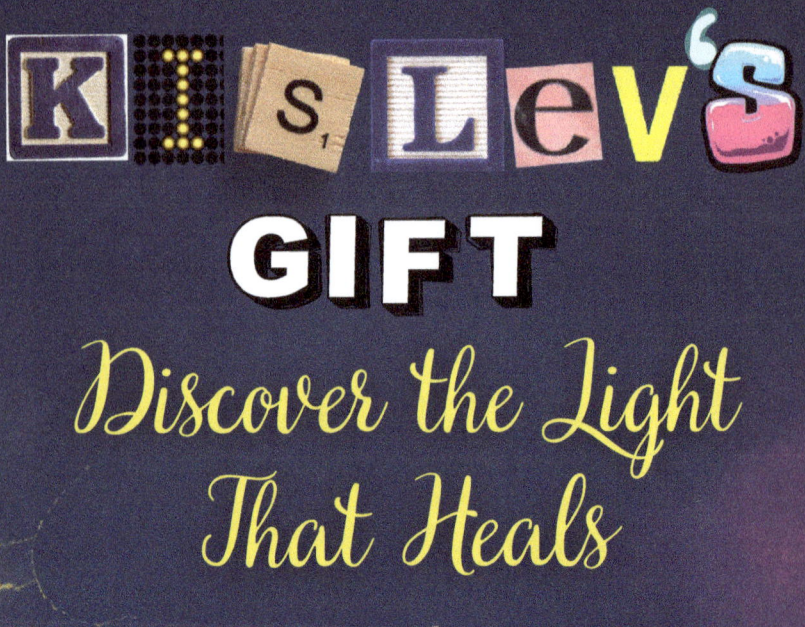

KISLEV'S GIFT

Discover the Light That Heals

Devorah Kur

Kislev arrives in the stillness of winter's darkness, when the days grow short and the nights are long and cold. Yet within this stillness lies a quiet invitation—to deepen our faith, trust and resilience. These dark nights, echoing the shadows of our history, whisper of hope and remind me of Anne Frank's luminous words: "Look at how a single candle can both defy and define the darkness."

There is something profoundly comforting about a candle glowing against the cold—a simple light that holds both warmth and promise.

This is the essence of Chanukah, which shines in the heart of Kislev, when we kindle flames to dispel the darkness and awaken our inner light and faith.

Each year, as Kislev returns, I pause to reflect on the challenges and blessings in my life, drawing strength from its resilient energy and from the steady faith that Hashem's light is always near, even if I can't always feel it.

According to *Sefer Yetzirah*, each Hebrew month carries a unique energy expressed through a letter, a tribe, a zodiac sign, a body part, and a human sense. Kislev, the ninth month, inspires us with themes around faith, trust, and resilience.

- **Kislev's letter:** Samech (ס) means "support," recalling the verse from Tehillim (145:14): "God supports (סוֹמֵךְ) all the fallen."

- **Its tribe:** Benjamin, beloved of God and whose territory was designated as home to the Temple, embodying both trust and rest: "Between his shoulders He rests." (Deuteronomy 33:12)

- **Its zodiac sign:** Sagittarius, with the bow (keshet)—both the rainbow of divine promise and the archer's bow of the Maccabees, symbolizing courage and trust.

- **The body part:** The stomach, representing intuition—a "gut knowing" that perceives truth beyond intellect.

- **Its sense:** Sleep, the deep rest that comes only from faith in God's providence: "And you shall lie down without fear." (Leviticus 26:6)

Together, these symbols reveal Kislev as a time to lean into Divine support, awaken courage, and discover that healing and light can be found within darkness. How fitting, then, that Chanukah begins in Kislev—a month filled with depth that goes way beyond doughnuts!

Chanukah is a time when we prevailed against the mighty Greek army, light shone through darkness, and the miracle of oil illuminated the Temple for eight days.

Beyond history, Chanukah serves as a spiritual guide, inviting us to discover resilience, deepen faith, and awaken the hidden healing spark within. Just as Hashem safeguarded the tiny flask of pure oil, He guards a spark of wholeness inside each of us, waiting to be uncovered, renewed, and kindled.

The miracle was not only that the oil lasted eight days, but that pure oil was found at all—hidden and preserved by an unknown Kohen. His nameless act teaches us that even small, unseen efforts can ripple outward, resulting in miracles. So too, as women, we daily perform countless unnoticed actions, like this Kohen, that sustain those around us—often not realizing the big impact we have.

The number eight, central to Chanukah, points us beyond the natural cycle of seven. Seven represents the physical order of creation (seven days of the week), while eight signifies transcendence (Brit Mila on the eighth day)—the eternal.

The Hebrew word for eight (שמונה) shares roots with שמן (oil) and נשמה (soul), both reminders that the essence of Chanukah is about rising above the ordinary and touching our soul within.

Lighting the Chanukah candles is more than a commemoration. **The Holy Arizal**, Kabbalist Rabbi Yitzchak Luria taught that the 613 mitzvot correspond to the 613 parts of the body, each bringing healing to its respective part.

Though not among the 613 mitzvot from the Torah, this mitzvah nourishes the whole body and soul, infusing Divine light into our being.

The timing of the candle-lighting is also significant. As night falls, we strike a flame, bringing light into the darkness.

Perek Shira teaches us that everything in creation has a purpose—for us to learn something from it.

Daylight teaches about kindness and clarity of vision, while night teaches about faith in the dark where we don't see clearly.

(Tehillim 92): להגיד בבקר חסדך ואמונתך בלילות — "To declare Your kindness in the morning and Your faithfulness at night." Life, too, alternates between clarity and confusion, joy and challenge.

Chanukah reminds us that even in difficulty, holiness emerges where we least expect it.

By attuning ourselves to this rhythm, we learn to uncover hope in adversity and strength in vulnerability, as the Maccabees did when they were few in number and fought anyway.

Recently, I was privileged to hear Omer Shem Tov (rescued hostage after 505 days) speak.

He said that during his captivity, there was a stretch of 50 continuous days in which he was submerged in darkness, kept in a small space in a tunnel where he could not even stand up or stretch his arms. In these 50 dark days, he said he felt tremendous spiritual light around him.

Rabbi Yaacov Haber notes that light often appears precisely where it is least expected. The Maccabees, few in number, overcame mighty forces.

Their courage demonstrates that faith and persistence can transform impossible circumstances.

Fire itself offers the same lesson: it always rises upward; it defies gravity, no matter how small.

So too, the Jewish people have persisted through exiles and persecution, rising up resiliently time and again —just as we are currently doing now.

Chanukah is thus not only a story of ancient victory, but a living reminder that our smallest acts of faith matter, and that once again, we rose up with resilience when there was little hope.

This Kislev, may we allow the light of Chanukah to enter our own darkness, and extend to all those in *Am Yisrael* who have suffered greatly. May we draw strength from the hidden spark Hashem has placed within each of us, finding healing in body, mind, and *neshama*. And may we share that light outward, illuminating not only our homes, but the world around us.

Devorah Kur is s a Logotherapist, SEP, IFS Level 3 practitioner, and Bereavement Counselor, who guides people through illness, grief, and trauma. Author of *Man's Search for Healing*, she weaves meaning, resilience, and post-traumatic growth into her work. At her Ra'anana Integrative Wellness clinic, she offers in-person and online sessions supporting healing of mind, body, and soul.

🌐 **dkwellness.co.il**

Finding My Flame—
From America to the Hills of Judea

BY RACHEL MOORE

I first came to Israel on a two-month high school trip through my youth group. I wasn't observant then, but I fell in love instantly. It wasn't rational or ideological—I just knew I was home.

A few months later, I came back during the Gulf War for my gap year. I wanted to see what life in Israel was really like and whether I could make it my home. My parents wanted me to finish college first, so I went to McGill University, where I studied English with a focus on Israel and Zionism. Those three years were all about preparing for *aliyah*—learning Hebrew, standing up for Israel on campus, and counting the days until I could return. When I finally graduated, I skipped the ceremony and flew straight to Jerusalem.

My first job was as the Assistant for Foreign Relations to the Mayor of Jerusalem—a real trial by fire. Those were the days when buses were exploding, and Prime Minister Rabin was assassinated. There was no internet, no Google, and no one in the office spoke English except the Mayor himself. It was sink or swim. I was desperate to learn before they discovered how little I knew.

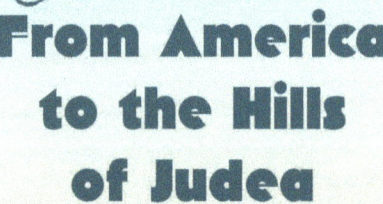

BEN GOLDSTEIN, CHANUKAH IN NEVE DANIEL, UNITY WARRIORS.ORG

But I did learn—everything from Hebrew to Israeli culture to how this country runs in chaos and faith at the same time.

I met incredible Israelis and several English-speaking families who invited me for *Shabbat* meals. They became my support system and remain treasured friends to this day. I lived in Old Katamon, surrounded by *Torah* classes, friends, and community. That's where I met my husband.

Years later, we moved to the U.S. for twelve years to raise my stepson after his mother relocated. It was a painful decision; I never wanted to leave Israel. But it was the right choice. We lived in a warm Orthodox community in New Jersey, yet I never truly felt I belonged. I yearned for Israel every single day.

That time taught me something I wish every Jew in the Diaspora could understand: **language builds identity.** My children grew up feeling fully Israeli because Hebrew was the language of our home, despite having no family in Israel or ever having lived there! It

reinforced how central Hebrew is to Jewish belonging.

When we finally returned, we realized we didn't fit into neat boxes. As American *baalei teshuva*, we didn't fully belong anywhere—so we built our own space. Speaking Hebrew helped us connect, build friendships, and truly become part of Israeli society. The families who once "adopted" me when I worked at City Hall are still part of our lives. My work in nonprofit PR lets me keep telling the stories of Israel's people, deepening my sense of purpose and belonging.

My relationship with *Hashem* has grown alongside my connection to this Land. There is no separation for me. *Hashem* blesses us through being here—working the Land and working on ourselves.

So much of my feminine Jewish identity comes from the women I've learned from here. I've had the privilege of working with remarkable role models: **Chantal Belzberg**, founder of OneFamily, helping victims of terror and

With Israel Prize winner and educator Miriam Peretz

their families; **Tzili Schneider**, founder of *Kesher Yehudi*, building Jewish unity and study partnerships; and **Naomi Stuchiner**, founder of *Beit Issie Shapiro*, who revolutionized inclusion for people with disabilities.

These women are modern-day heroines—steeped in *Torah*, changing the world with compassion and faith. I simply help tell their stories.

In my *yishuv*, Neve Daniel in Gush Etzion, the family-centered culture reinforces everything I value. My children are my greatest accomplishment, the best thing I ever did or will do. They inspire me daily, guiding my growth, my faith, and my joy. And my Israeli grandchildren? The best return on investment anyone could imagine.

PHOTO: COURTESY OF RACHEL MOORE

Advice for Women Dreaming of Aliyah

Learn Hebrew. Speak badly. Read children's books. Watch shows you barely understand. Make the shopkeepers talk to you in Hebrew. It's not just a language, it's your doorway into belonging.

Be ready to leave your comfort zone – and stay out of it. Israel isn't about being comfortable. *Hashem* placed this Land where rain is scarce so that we would learn to pray and work for it. Work the soil of your life here; something beautiful will grow.

And don't feel pressured to stop missing Sundays or your favorite childhood treat. Someone has to be the first. You're giving future generations the gift of not

being immigrants—because you were. Stumble, make mistakes, and know your great-great-grandchildren will thank you for it.

Community is not optional; it's part of being Jewish. I live in a small *yishuv* of fewer than 800 families, and everyone relies on each other. When you give, you show love. When you give in Israel, you start to love the people you didn't know—and you find yourself included in ways you never imagined. Ask for help constantly, and pay it forward. You'll always need both.

The Light of Chanukah

Chanukah is the epitome of Jewish strength; hope when things seem darkest, and light born from determination.

October 7th and its aftermath have taken a toll on all of us. I grew up believing "never again" meant something – that humanity had learned. But the world has regressed. My children are growing up with a deeper familiarity with evil than I ever did.

Every day in Israel feels like a *Chanukah* moment now—darkness met with light; Hostage parents keeping *Shabbat* after their children return home. Liat Haim forgiving the soldier who accidentally killed her son. Tali and Jair Eisenmann creating joy for sick children after losing their own. Miriam Fuld arming soldiers and strengthening *Am Yisrael* after her husband's murder.

Who is like Your people, *Hashem*? I tell the stories of people who have faced heartbreak and respond with love. They are all modern-day Maccabees—beaten down, small, and mighty.

I didn't grow up in a Jewish community. I was raised in a tiny New England town where I saw more deer than people. *Chanukah* reminds me that *this* is where Jews belong—in the Jewish homeland.

My oldest daughter was born on December 25th. When she was little and saw the decorations and lights from the non-Jewish holidays, I told her the neighbors heard it was her birthday. But *Chanukah* in Israel isn't about sweaters or blue-and-white decorations at Target. It's about knowing that even when darkness closes in, **we** are the light—the flame that keeps burning when the oil should have run out.

Around the world, *Chanukah* has become a cultural celebration, but the real message is the opposite: be distinct, strong, and proud. Be that single candle refusing to go out when the world demands you fit in. That's our calling—to be a light unto the nations.

Home in Every Hill

I have so many favorite places in Israel. *Breichat HaMishushim* up north feels magical, hidden in a nature reserve. But Jerusalem is my heart, my true love, my past and my future. Visiting the *Kotel* plaza and picturing our Holy Temple still gives me chills. *Ir David* connects me straight to our roots.

Every time I look out at Israel's rolling hills, I feel the same love I felt as a teenager. It's a running joke at home —whenever we drive anywhere, I ask the kids what we're looking at, and they have to answer: *"God's gift to the Jewish people."*

Thirty years later, I still feel that wonder and gratitude every day.

Rachel (Temkin) Moore grew up in New England, and made *aliyah* at 22. She lives in Neve Daniel with her husband Barak, is a mother of seven (one serving in Gaza), stepmother of one, and grandmother of two. She is CEO of **Moore Connected Communications**, a writer, and a speaker, who sings whenever she gets the chance.

🌐 mooreconnected.com

YES, YOU CAN:
Aliyah with Children with Autism

BY SHAINA SILVERMAN

"Is your son normal?"

It was a question asked innocently by a student of mine right before class was about to begin. He had seen me and my son at the park the afternoon prior and was genuinely curious if my son was "normal".

His question took me by surprise. My first instinct was to respond, "Of course he's normal! He's my adorable, four-year-old little boy, perfect in every way!"...but instead I replied, "He has autism." I smiled and added, "isn't he the cutest?", and proceeded to start the lesson.

At the time we hadn't really told anyone about the diagnosis. What started as a speech delay and other social/emotional challenges had eventually led us to a diagnosis— ASD (Autism Spectrum Disorder).

To borrow a phrase from our pre-*aliyah* life in Houston, Texas, "this wasn't our first rodeo." Our middle child was diagnosed with ASD about one year earlier. Receiving these diagnoses, and the experiences that followed, only solidified our belief that making *aliyah* and raising our family in Israel has been one of the best decisions we've ever made.

The Special Ed services our children receive here have been transformatively beneficial and full of "only-in-Israel" moments. In addition to the practical necessities, we've had the *z'chut* of meeting educators and therapists that view their roles through the lens of holy *shlichut* for these special *neshamot*. The fact that there are publicly-funded schools and classrooms designated as "*tikshoret*" (ASD) that provide our children with the services they need in our Jewish homeland is truly a miracle.

IF YOU ARE A FAMILY CONSIDERING ALIYAH WITH A CHILD ON THE SPECTRUM HERE ARE SOME TIPS AND SUGGESTIONS TO HELP YOU.

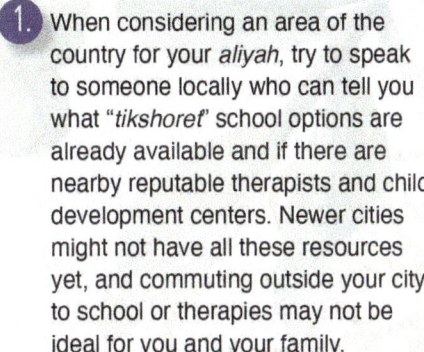 1. When considering an area of the country for your *aliyah*, try to speak to someone locally who can tell you what "*tikshoret*" school options are already available and if there are nearby reputable therapists and child development centers. Newer cities might not have all these resources yet, and commuting outside your city to school or therapies may not be ideal for you and your family.

2. Join local and/or national support groups. Facebook groups like **"ASD kids in Israel"** contain a wealth of resources, advice, inspiration and a healthy dose of venting (and an even healthier dose of compassionate responses). Your local tribe of ASD parents is often happy to help newcomers who are just starting to navigate the city's health and education systems.

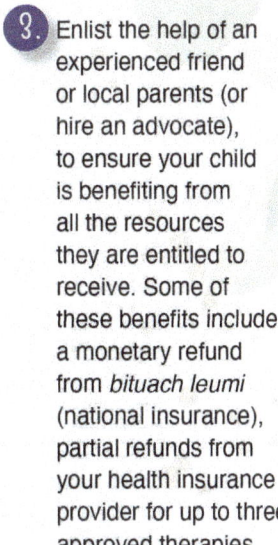 3. Enlist the help of an experienced friend or local parents (or hire an advocate), to ensure your child is benefiting from all the resources they are entitled to receive. Some of these benefits include a monetary refund from *bituach leumi* (national insurance), partial refunds from your health insurance provider for up to three approved therapies

ILLUSTRATION BY DENA ACKERMAN

Dena Ackerman

per week (psychology, OT, speech, etc.), an exemption from waiting in lines, as well as discounts on car registration, property tax and various museums and attractions throughout the country.

Raising children with ASD is challenging. Raising children with ASD in Israel has been an opportunity to appreciate our blessings and feel that we are exactly where we are meant to be. *Baruch Hashem*, Israel is a country that provides the resources our children need. We have an incredible support system that goes beyond family. It's here that we feel most comfortable sharing our challenges, our journey and our miracle moments with others. And that's way better than just "normal".

Shaina Silverman made aliyah to Rechovot with her family in 2017. She has nearly 20 years experience in education. Shaina now works as a certified Jewish CBT therapist and life coach. She is passionate about helping children overcome anxiety and guiding them in finding their unique gifts and talents while strengthening their self-confidence.

✉ smileCBT@gmail.com

REHOVOT

Rooted in History, Growing Toward the Future

PHOTO SHANA SILVERMAN

BY ADINA FREUD

 OUR DRIVE HOME

It was July 31, 2019, midday. I found myself sitting in a *hasa'ah* with fifteen bags of luggage, somewhere between exhaustion and disbelief. Like so many others before me, I had turned my dream into reality—moving my family (my husband and three young kids) to Israel, officially making *Aliyah*.

As I drifted in and out of sleep, I caught sight of six tall flagpoles waving large Israeli flags in the distance. The driver pointed and said, "You see that? That's Rehovot."

Something about those flags struck me—the pride, the rootedness, the quiet strength of this city. I've driven that same road hundreds of times since, and every time I approach Rehovot, I feel that same sense of coming home.

WHY REHOVOT?

To be candid, this is the question I'm asked most often: Why Rehovot?

For us, the decision came down to two things—family and education. My brother had made *Aliyah* to Rehovot three years earlier and spoke warmly of the city, its people, and the lifestyle. That connection mattered.

At the time, our oldest child was seven and needed a special-education communication class. Through research—and countless WhatsApp conversations with parents already living here—it became clear that Rehovot had the programs, professionals, and compassion we were looking for. It wasn't just about finding services; it was about finding a community that understood.

That's something you quickly learn in this city: Rehovot may be large, but its heart feels small and close.

FINDING THE ANGLO HEART OF THE CITY

Most Anglo *olim* in Rehovot live within a few kilometers of one another, forming a strong hub of connection. We chose a neighborhood within that 2-3 km radius—close to public transportation, the train, Main Street (food and shopping), the mall, the Weizmann Institute, and great parks.

When people talk about "where they fit," two shuls often come up: Berman, an Anglo Modern Orthodox/*Dati Leumi* community, and *Chatam*, an Anglo *Yeshivish/Haredi* one. But the beauty of Rehovot is that belonging isn't confined by shul walls. The lines blur easily. Families cross paths, children play together, and friendships grow organically.

Other *shuls* like Beit Heimfeld and Mercaz Avraham add to this sense of connection, each attracting their own mix of Israelis and Anglos. What

defines the Anglo presence here isn't uniformity—it's warmth, openness, and a willingness to show up for one another.

THE WORD ON THE STREET

Walk through Rehovot and you'll hear Hebrew on every corner—it's distinctly Israeli, rooted and real. Yet somehow, you'll also hear the familiar rhythm of English woven through daily life.

That mix captures what I love most about living here. Rehovot encourages integration—it gently pushes *olim* to adapt, to learn the language, to belong—while still giving space for comfort and familiarity.

Religious life spans the full spectrum: secular, traditional, and religious families live side by side. The diversity creates tolerance, not tension. For Anglos, that means you can find your place without having to fit a mold.

A CITY ON THE MOVE

Rehovot has blossomed into a hub of education, science, and culture. Anchored by the Weizmann Institute and Kaplan Hospital, the city continues to grow—new neighborhoods, cafés, and shops open constantly.

One of the most exciting developments is the upcoming Blue Line train, which will connect Rehovot directly to Tel Aviv. It's a sign of the city's direction—forward-thinking but still grounded in community.

For *olim*, Rehovot offers the perfect mix: suburban comfort with the energy and opportunity of a city that's alive and expanding.

PHOTO ADINA FREUD

 BUILDING ROOTS

For families, Rehovot offers countless ways to connect. The two main gathering spots for Anglo parents are Shkolnick Park near Chatam and Meltzer Park near Berman. On Shabbat afternoons, both fill with the laughter of children and the hum of parents catching up in English, Hebrew, or both.

And then there's what I like to call Rehovot's "invisible web" of connection—our WhatsApp groups. The *Neshei* Rehovot chat, in particular, has become a lifeline for so many. It's where you can ask anything: where to buy school shoes, how to pay a doctor insurance payment authorization, or who to call for a plumber. It's not just about information—it's about kindness, responsiveness, and community in motion.

There's an unspoken rule among the Anglo *olim* here: we prioritize connection over comparison. The emphasis isn't on who fits where, but on how we can help each other.

 REHOVOT: THE CITY OF SCIENCE AND SPIRIT

Rehovot is known as the "City of Science," but anyone who lives here knows it's equally a city of heart.

The Weizmann Institute is a national treasure—not only a center of scientific excellence but also one of the most beautiful green spaces in the country. Its tree-lined paths, open lawns, and tranquil gardens make it a local gem for walks and picnics.

Nearby, Park HaHadarim is another favorite. It's spacious, filled with fruit trees, picnic tables, and even peacocks roaming around a large duck pond. A small coffee truck adds to the charm, making it a perfect place to unwind.

For summer fun, the Weisgal Community Pool offers clean facilities, separate swimming hours, and a friendly local crowd—simple pleasures that make daily life here feel balanced.

The city's mayor, Matan Dil, has brought renewed energy and care to Rehovot. Under his leadership, the city has grown cleaner, greener, and more family-friendly,

with frequent cultural events, public improvements, and a focus on education.

SHIURIM AND SHARED SPACES

Rehovot offers many opportunities for *Torah* learning and meaningful gatherings. Both Chatam and Berman run regular *shiurim*, classes, and community programs that bridge generations and backgrounds.

For women, *Rosh Chodesh* gatherings and parenting workshops offer connection and growth in a warm, supportive environment. Recently, I launched The Rehovot Round Table—a space where people can speak openly and feel seen in their challenges. The goal is simple: to remind each other that none of us are truly alone.

EDUCATION

When it comes to education, Rehovot's options for Anglo families are diverse and high-quality. These are some of the schools most popular among *olim*:

For Boys (Elementary):
Etz Chaim Banim — *Mamlachti Haredi*
Talmud Torah HaRAY"aH —
  Rav Kook *Dati Leumi Torani*
Noam Banim — *Dati Leumi Torani*
Tachkemoni and Bereishit —
  Co-Ed *Dati Leumi, Bereishit*
  with a democratic approach
Chabad Banim — *Mamlachti Haredi*

For Girls (Elementary):
P'ninim — *Mamlachti Haredi*,
  with a progressive spirit
Noam Banot — *Dati Leumi Torani*
Chabad Banot — *Mamlachti Haredi*
Beit Yaakov — *Haredi*

High School (Boys):
Yeshivat Hadarom
Yeshivat Amit Amichai
Yeshivat Amit Hammer — advanced
  Kodesh and *Dati Leumi* tracks

High School (Girls):
Tzviya — *Dati Leumi*
Amit Hallel — *Dati Leumi*
Beit Yaakov — *Haredi*
Pelech — *Dati Leumi*

FINDING HOME

For us, Rehovot became more than an address—it became a reflection of our values. It's where integration meets individuality, where people look out for each other, and where every small act of kindness reminds you that belonging isn't something you're given—it's something you build, one connection at a time.

Adina Freud is a U.S.-trained Physician Associate, entrepreneur, public speaker, *Kallah* teacher, and super-connector. She made *Aliyah* from the U.S. in 2019 with her husband and children and is now a proud mother of five. Adina founded Aliyah Prime Medical to bring peace of mind to *olim* and created The Rehovot Round Table, bringing people together through empathy, connection, and strength.

PHOTO BY AVI JACOB

WALK IN THE FOOTSTEPS OF THE MACCABEES:
5 SITES TO VISIT THIS CHANUKAH

BY TALI GUIGUI

This *Chanukah*, when you light your *menorah* and spin the *dreidel*, imagine standing in the actual places where it all happened.

For 2,000 years, Jews spun *dreidels* with the letters *nun-gimmel-heh-shin: Nes Gadol Hayah Sham*—a great miracle happened there. Today, in Israel, we spin dreidels with the letters *nun-gimmel-heh-peh: Nes Gadol Hayah Poh*—a great miracle happened here. Here—where we live today. Here—in the same land as our ancestors, the Maccabees.

The *Chanukah* story isn't just ancient history—it's written into Israel's landscape. These five sites trace the path of the revolt from its beginning in Modi'in through the battles that led to Jerusalem, where the Temple was reclaimed and the *menorah* lit once again.

1. UMM EL-UMDAN (MODI'IN): WHERE IT ALL BEGAN

The hills of ancient Modi'in are where it all started. The Greeks had outlawed *Shabbat, Torah* study, and circumcision—systematically dismantling Jewish life. When they arrived in Modi'in, they gathered the Jews, built an altar, and demanded they sacrifice a pig to the Greek gods.

Matityahu was a respected priest and elder. The Greeks offered him money and status to go first and set an example. He refused. Instead, another Jew stepped forward to comply. That's when Matityahu killed both the collaborator and the Greek officer. In front of the whole town, he shouted: "Whoever is zealous for *Hashem*, follow me!" He and his five sons— *Yehuda, Yonatan, Shimon, Yochanan,* and *Elazar*—ran for the hills, and the revolution had officially begun.

Today, you can walk among the ruins of this ancient village, including what may be the oldest synagogue ever discovered in Israel—a 2,200-year-old floor where Jews gathered to pray and perhaps to plan the uprising. The ancient *mikveh* still stands, along with burial sites and the caves where the Maccabees first hid.

Picture it: Jewish families actually lived here during the *Chanukah* story. They used these doorways, these cisterns. Today, Israelis pass this site on their daily commutes without a second thought. Yet this is where the *Chanukah* story began more than 2,000 years ago.

Bet Horon

PHOTO: AI GENERATED

2. MATAT OBSERVATION POINT (BET HORON): THE VICTORY THAT CHANGED EVERYTHING

Word of the revolt spread quickly. The Greeks sent Governor Seron with a professional army to crush what they thought was a minor uprising. He had superior numbers, better training, and the best soldiers in the world. But *Yehuda HaMaccabee* knew these hills like the back of his hand.

The pass at Bet Horon is narrow and winding, flanked by steep slopes— perfect for an ambush. The Maccabees struck hard, killing Seron in the first assault. When their commander fell, the Greek soldiers panicked and fled.

From the observation point today, you can see exactly why Yehuda chose this spot. The terrain tells the story. Sometimes you don't need the bigger army—you need to know the ground. After this victory, the Greeks had to take the Maccabees seriously.

Kever Shmuel Hanavi

3. NEBI SAMUEL (MIZPAH): THE HIGH GROUND

The Greeks responded by sending 60,000 soldiers and horsemen. *Yehuda* pulled back to Mizpah, one of the highest peaks in the region. You can see for miles in every direction—strategic ground where the prophet Shmuel once judged Israel.

Archaeologists have uncovered an entire *Hasmonean* quarter here—rows of buildings where Jewish families lived during the *Chanukah* story. These aren't just ruins. They're homes where Jewish families lived during the revolt, watching history unfold.

But Mizpah was more than strategic high ground. This was where the prophet Shmuel gathered Israel to fast and pray in times of crisis. The Maccabees knew this. They chose Mizpah precisely because it was a place where Israel had always turned to *HaShem* when everything seemed lost. They fasted, prayed, and sought divine help before facing the Greek army.

Then *Yehuda* made a bold decision: don't wait for the Greeks to attack— strike first. Under cover of night, the Maccabees hit the Greek camp and won another crucial victory. Years later, *Yehuda* returned to this same mountain before the battle where he killed the Greek general Nicanor.

4. MITZPOR HABANIM (ALON SHVUT): THE BATTLE OF THE ELEPHANTS

After three years of fighting, the Maccabees reclaimed Jerusalem and rededicated the Temple. But the war continued.

Two years later, the Greeks returned with everything they had: a massive army and 32 war elephants. Near *Bet*

Zecharia, just north of this viewpoint, *Yehuda's* brother *Elazar* saw what he thought was the king's elephant. He ran beneath it and stabbed it from below. The elephant fell—crushing *Elazar* to death. A nearby community bears his name today.

This time, the Maccabees lost. They retreated to Jerusalem and the Greeks besieged the city. Food ran out. Just when it seemed hopeless, political chaos back in the Seleucid capital forced the Greek general to abandon the siege and rush home. Jerusalem was saved by circumstances beyond anyone's control.

The Maccabees didn't win every fight. But they held on. And sometimes, just holding on is enough.

5. YAAKOV'S DREAM SITE (BET EL): WHERE THE STORY COMES FULL CIRCLE

Following the start of the revolt in Modi'in, *Matityahu* and his sons fled to the mountains around Bet El, hiding in caves throughout these hills. This is where our forefather *Yaakov* dreamed of angels ascending and descending a ladder to heaven—a place already layered with Jewish memory. These mountains saw the Maccabees transform from refugees into warriors.

Matityahu led the rebellion for about a year before he died and was buried in Modi'in, passing leadership to his son *Yehuda*. Six years after the Temple was reclaimed, these mountain passes saw *Yehuda's* last battle. In the Battle of

Umm-El Umdam (Modi'in)

PHOTO BY HOWIE MISCHEL

Elasa, he and his most loyal warriors fell fighting a much larger Greek army.

He didn't live to see full independence, but what he started—the fight for Jewish sovereignty, the refusal to give up our identity—continued through his brothers.

The view from *Bet El* stretches for miles. Knowing that *Yehuda* fought his last battle here, that he died without seeing the final victory, makes the story real. He didn't need to see the ending to believe it was worth fighting for.

A NoTE ABOUT JERUSALEM

The heart of the *Chanukah* story unfolds in Jerusalem—the siege, the liberation, the rededication of the Temple, and the miracle of the oil. Jerusalem deserves its own visit, its own exploration. Whether you stand at the *Kotel*, walk through the Jewish Quarter, or visit the archaeological sites, you're seeing where it all culminated.

The five sites in this article trace the journey to Jerusalem—the battles that made the miracle of the oil possible. Because before there could be a miracle of oil, there had to be a miracle of survival: a small group of Jews defeating the world's greatest army.

WHY THESE SiTES MATTER ToDAY

After the Maccabees defeated the Greeks, Jews enjoyed about a century of independence before the Romans came. In 70 CE, the Romans destroyed the Second Temple and exiled nearly all the Jewish inhabitants across their empire. For two millennia, Jews lived

scattered in foreign lands, dreaming of the day they could return.

Our ancestors in exile could only imagine these hills. Today, you can walk them.

This *Chanukah*, don't just read the story—walk it. Stand where *Matityahu* shouted "Follow me!" See why *Yehuda* chose that narrow pass. Climb to Mizpah where our ancestors prayed before impossible battles. These aren't museum pieces behind glass. They're mountains you can hike, ruins you can touch, views you can see with your own eyes.

For generations, we said the miracle happened there. Now we can say it happened here.

Chanukah Sameach!

Tali Guigui is a Tour Guide in Israel and Jewish History Educator who brings ancient stories to life through the land where they happened. Her passion is helping people see themselves as part of our people's story—as the next link in the chain of thousands of years of Jewish existence. She lives in Jerusalem—her favorite city in the world—with her husband and two daughters.

 @trippinwithtali

From Strangers to Sisters

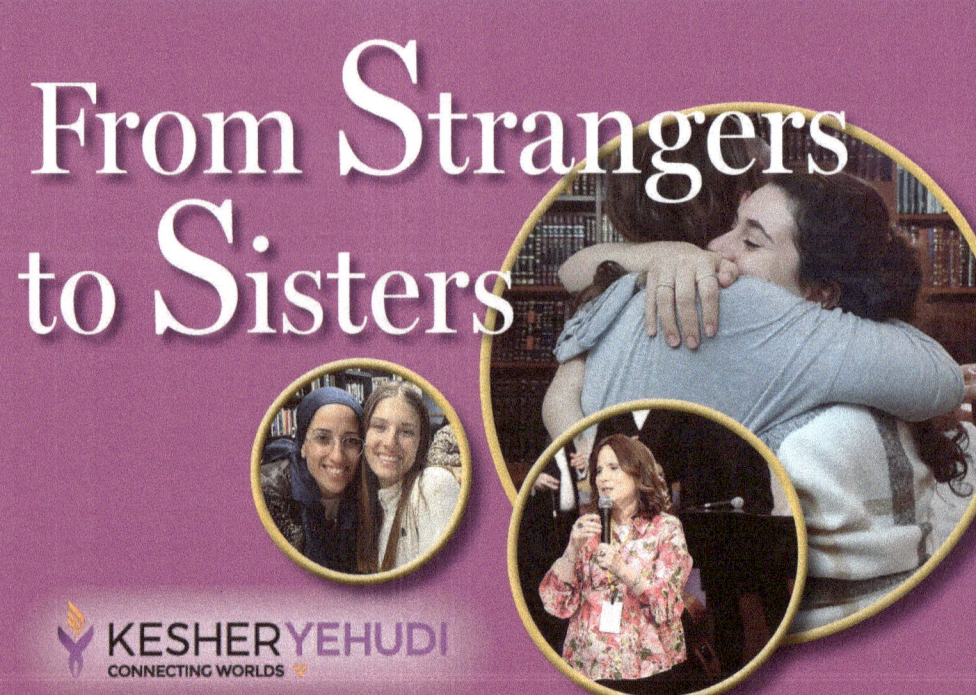

KESHER YEHUDI
CONNECTING WORLDS

Tzili Schneider's Visionary Movement Reuniting Am Yisrael

BY RAY ELISHA

TZILI SCHNEIDER IS MAKING GREAT STRIDES in the world of *achdut*. She founded Kesher Yehudi, a movement that sparks relationships between all different types of Jews by learning in a *chevruta*, sharing *Shabbat* meals, and cultivating conversations between those who otherwise might have never connected.

"I was riding the same bus every morning as another woman for four years," explained Tzili. "She was not religious. I was. We never spoke. I sat there and thought, 'how did we let it come to this? We are both mothers, neighbors, Jews, and we're strangers?' I realized that the walls between us were growing too high."

"I created Kesher Yehudi to create one-on–one *chevruta* pairs between *Haredi* and secular Jews in order to connect through the one thing that belongs to us all equally: the *Torah*."

Over time, Kesher Yehudi has grown significantly, with participants ranging from soldiers to rabbis, to Nova survivors to businessmen. Today, it has over 16,000 participants. When it comes to *chevruta* learning, Tzili makes matches by pairing people with shared interests, curiosity, and openness.

"Each pair begins with structure such as guided topics and learning materials. The most important rule is to listen before you speak. Don't try to change the other person. Try to know them," she exclaimed. "Respect grows from there."

The religious volunteers are also prepared to be learners, not teachers. She explained that the volunteers learn to accompany their learning partner in their pain without trying to erase it. Many of the Nova survivors involved in Kesher Yehudi didn't feel ready for therapy the first year after October 7th, and the volunteers being there for them as a loving presence and companion was a huge help.

> ❝ **What unites us isn't uniformity, but shared identity. One people, one Torah, one destiny.** ❞

"The *Torah* is not a product to sell. It is our shared inheritance," Tzili stated. "Every Jew has a chelek in *Torah*, whether they know it yet or not."

Tzili has connected with many Nova survivors and their families over the past two years. When asked to share transformative or healing stories she's witnessed, she responded, "There are thousands. Matan Angrest's parents have been learning with me for over a year. All that time they had no idea that their son was learning and davening in captivity. Immediately upon his return, he asked for *tefillin*, which I had the honor of bringing to him!"

PHOTO: DAVID WEILL

PHOTO: SHLOMI COHEN

Tzili Schneider on the left with
Orly Gilboa, mother of
former hostage Daniela Gilboa

"What unites us isn't uniformity, but shared identity. One people, one *Torah*, one destiny. When people say it's too late, we're too divided, I invite them to come sit in on a *chevruta*. See the Breslover sitting with a tattooed executive learning about kindness in Pirkei *Avot*. Watch the respect, curiosity, and laughter."

Reminiscing about what happened right before the start of the war, Tzili talked about a terrible incident that happened in Tel Aviv on *Yom Kippur.* "The open minyan that hundreds come to each year was disrupted because of the *mechitza*. All of the fighting and anger fomented by the judicial reform and other political issues came to damage our connection to God. On *Yom Kippur* — one of the

Tzili also stated that a survivor of the Nova festival came to a *Shabbat* organized by Kesher Yehudi and said that *Shabbat* was the first time she'd slept through the night since October 7th.

"We don't preach. We don't fix. We hold space. We do not offer or in any way try to replace real professional emotional help. We are trying to give help in the means that regular people can, by reaching out to our fellow brothers and sisters with dignity, warmth, and spiritual sincerity."

Tzili then spoke about *hashgacha pratit* and the first *Shabbat* hosted by Kesher Yehudi, that included hostage families.

"None of us knew what to expect. We cried and prayed together and held each other. Two days later, the first hostages were released. That moment reminded us that when we stop fighting and start uniting, something shifts in heaven."

PHOTO: SHLOMI COHEN

Shelly Shem Tov on the left, mother of
former hostage Omer Shem Tov
with her *chavruta*.

days that most Israelis still share! When Shelley Shem Tov was screaming on camera about achdut with a broken heart, I felt compelled to go to Hostage Square and hug her. Then I decided, when I met her and the other families that were suffering, to invite them to keep one full *Shabbat* in the merit of their loved ones."

When discussing a connection between the miracle of *Chanukah* and the work that Kesher Yehudi does, Tzili told us that the *Chanukah* light is a kind of light that comes from faith when logic says to give up, and that her work is the same.

"In *chevruta* pairs, at *Shabbat* tables, in homes, we light one flame, then another, and another. Just like *Chanukah*, it spreads. One small jar of oil…eight days. One *chevruta*…thousands of friendships."

Looking into the future, Tzili has a dream that Kesher Yehudi will become a basic part of Israeli culture. That every Jew should have a *chevruta*. She is also in the process of building an English-language track.

"The real goal is cultural. We want to change the instinctive reaction people have when they meet someone 'different.' Not suspicion or judgment, but curiosity, respect, and love."

If you would like to become involved with Kesher Yehudi, Tzili encourages becoming involved with or sponsoring a *chevruta*. You can also invite Kesher Yehudi to your community or school to bring the model to you.

Tzili Schneider is the founder of Kesher Yehudi, a social movement uniting secular and religious Jews through *Torah* study and deep personal connection. Under her leadership, Kesher Yehudi has matched thousands of *chavruta* pairs across Israel, earning national recognition and the Jerusalem Unity Prize. She lives in Jerusalem and speaks globally on unity, Jewish identity, and spiritual resilience.

🌐 **kesher-yehudi.com/en**

Ray Elisha is a writer whose dream is to one day own a communal bookstore and to live on a large plot of land. Here, she envisions rehabilitating animals, offering vegan education and cooking classes, and raising a tribe of loving, wandering children, all guided by her deep connection to Israel and Judaism.

Oil & Soul: The Fragrance That Heals

BY CHANA FRAZIN

As we prepare to celebrate *Chanukah* and the miracle of the oil that burned for eight days, I want to share another aspect of oils with you—essential oils.

Often known simply for bringing pleasant scents into the home, these powerful plant molecules hold much deeper potential.

To understand the depth of essential oils, we need to go back to the very beginning—to *Parashat Bereishit*, to *chet ha'rishon*, the first sin in the Garden of Eden. *Adam* and *Chava* were told not to eat from the Tree in the center of the Garden—but they did. We know the story well: the snake, the deception, the shame. In one moment, humankind fell, and before the first *Shabbat* was complete, they were sent out of *Gan Eden*.

Four of the five senses were involved in this transgression. *Chava* saw the fruit, she heard the snake, she touched it, and together they ate from it. Yet one sense is strikingly absent from the story—smell. *Chazal* teach us that the sense of smell was untouched by sin and therefore remains completely pure.

Centuries later, science uncovered something remarkable: our sense of smell is unique among the senses. While other sensory signals travel through filters and processing centers in the brain, scent molecules travel directly and unblocked to the limbic system—the emotional and memory center of the brain. Within less than a minute of inhaling, the aroma begins to influence mood, memory, and emotion. What our sages knew spiritually, science is now confirming.

So what does it mean for us today that our sense of smell is pure? It means we have a direct line to a part of ourselves that remains whole and unblemished. Essential oils—highly concentrated aromatic extracts from plants—have the ability to reach us at that deepest level. Over the years, I have witnessed again and again the blessings they bring, both for physical and emotional healing.

I have worked with children and adults struggling with anger, fear, anxiety, or sadness. Introducing aroma during difficult moments can shift the atmosphere almost instantly. The oils interrupt patterns of reactive behavior and, through consistent daily use, can help build new neural pathways that support transformation at the core.

Chana Frazin

One particularly powerful practice is called aromatic anchoring—linking a specific aroma to a desired emotional or spiritual state. Just as the smell of freshly baked chocolate chip cookies might transport you back to your grandmother's kitchen, an essential oil can be intentionally paired with feelings of calm, gratitude, or joy. Later, smelling that same oil allows the body to "recall" and re-enter that state. In this way, oils become tools of memory, healing, and transformation.

The *Torah* gives us a profound example of the healing power of fragrance. After the rebellion of *Korach*, a devastating plague swept through the people. *Moshe* instructed *Aharon* to take the *ketoret*—the sacred incense—and run into the midst of the camp. The verse tells us, "He stood between the living and the dead, and the plague was stopped" (*Bamidbar* 17:13). Our sages teach that the *ketoret* possessed a unique power—both spiritual and physical—to bring purification and healing. In that moment, incense—fragrance—literally saved lives.

The *ketoret* was a carefully crafted blend of eleven spices, each chosen with intention. It carried both beauty and potency, bridging heaven and earth, body and soul. Today, while we no longer have the *ketoret* in our *Beit HaMikdash*, we still have access to the natural gift of aroma through essential oils. They remind us that scent is not just pleasant—it is transformative.

Each oil has its own unique personality and message, offering gentle guidance for the heart and soul. For example:

Frankincense— Known as the oil of truth and spirituality, frankincense— called Levona in Hebrew—was used in the Ketoret and is the most frequently mentioned spice throughout the Tanach. Derived from tree resin, it is grounding, calming, and supports meditation, clear breathing, and focus. Frankincense reminds us that true wellness is both physical and spiritual.

Ginger with its spiciness creates movement rather than sitting back and letting life pass you by. Ginger puts you in the driver's seat of your life. A great oil to use diluted on the solar plexus, a place of personal power & confidence.

Blue Tansy is the oil of inspired action. Feeling stuck or overwhelmed by new beginnings? Blue Tansy helps ignite your spark and gives you the gentle push to take action. It helps turn your ideas and passions into clear, doable steps.

Chana Frazin is a certified aromatherapist with over a decade of experience in science- and research-based essential oil use. As a certified Essential Emotions Coach, she integrates Jewish wisdom with proven aromatherapy practices to support emotional and spiritual growth. Chana is the founder of The Oil for Me, a family-run business. She teaches both in person and on Zoom, empowering women to bring natural solutions into their homes and become their own "Dr. Mom."

⊕ TheOilforMe.com

EMMUNITY:
THE LIGHT WITHIN

BY ITA TEIGMAN

On *Chanukah*, we celebrate our Divine resilience. We celebrate the light of *Torah*, the light of *Emunah*, and the light of making conscious choices.

Great health, to me, means a special kind of resilience—the trademark of *Hashem*'s precious children.

It's what I call EMMUNITY: our *Emunah* (faith) and Unity as the foundation of body, mind, and soul resilience.

It's also a powerful acronym—a guide to help us build strong physical and emotional health, prevent illness (especially in winter), and recover quickly when the sniffles or coughs appear despite our best efforts.

> **Actually, we were created to desire power—not power over others, but power within ourselves.**

EMPOWERED

You've heard it said: "Knowledge is power." Why would you want power?

Actually, we were created to desire power—not power over others, but power within ourselves.

Power to feel vibrant and strong. Power to take responsibility for our nefesh ha-behamit (animal soul).

Being empowered means being open to learning from those who thrive—to observe, to ask, to grow, and to refine our habits. When we choose nourishing foods, meaningful movement, refined thoughts, and deep connection to Hashem, create true EMMUNITY.

EMMUNITY

E EMPOWERED

M MICROBIOME, MITOCHONDRIA, METHYLATION

M MOVEMENT

U UNLIMITED ABUNDANCE & HEALING MINDSET

N NUTRITION & NATURE

I IMMUNE SYSTEM SUPPORT, INHALATION TO CLEANSE SINUSES

T THOUGHTS BECOME YOUR REALITY & FUEL EMOTION

Y MY BIG "Y": AS A UNIQUELY DIVINELY BELOVED INDIVIDUAL, A LIVING REPRESENTATIVE OF THE ALMIGHTY

MICROBIOME, MITOCHONDRIA, METHYLATION

These three concepts are crucial to our overall health and well-being—especially for staying really well through the winter months.

Microbiome refers to the vast population of microscopic organisms (bacteria, fungi, viruses, and parasites) that sustain our bodies. When balanced, they help digest food, manufacture vitamins, and support immunity.

Feed your microbiome with prebiotic foods, and add fermented foods like dairy, vegetables, grains, or nuts. Avoid ultra-processed foods, which fuel harmful bacteria and trigger cravings for more of the same.

Mitochondria are the "power plants" of our cells. They thrive on a clean diet rich in vegetables, sprouts, quality proteins, and movement that builds muscle and supports circulation.

Methylation is the detox process of our cells—essential in today's toxin-filled world. Our bodies were designed for real, whole foods, not chemical substitutes. Clean eating helps your cells do their job as *Hashem* intended.

MOVEMENT

Do you sit most of the day? Research shows that **"sitting is the new smoking."**

We must work—but also move! Try "exercise snacks": short 2–5-minute breaks every hour or two for squats, jumping jacks, or mini-trampoline rebounding. Movement boosts circulation, metabolism, and energy—key ingredients for health and joy.

UNLIMITED HEALING MINDSET

Hashem exhorts us: **"Choose Life."**

Our birthright is life, health, and vitality—yet society teaches us to fear illness and decline. We can stay stuck in fear, or we can choose *emunah*: that *Hashem* is *Hakol Yachol*—capable of anything.

What we focus on grows. Developing a "kosher meditation" practice strengthens our subconscious belief in *Hashem's* infinite healing power.

NUTRITION & NATURE

As the Rambam taught, *"Let food be your medicine and medicine be your food."* Proper eating is our responsibility.

If we harm our health through poor habits, we limit our ability to serve *Hashem*—and we are accountable for that.

Healthy food prep can be learned through workshops or videos. It's not complicated—it just takes love and awareness. Eat calmly, eat mindfully, and remember: nourishing yourself is an act of self-love and gratitude to the One Who provides.

Nature, too, is our healer. Whether on a mountain trail, at the sea, or walking barefoot on the earth (grounding), *Hashem's* creation recharges our energy. Step outside. Breathe. It's all from Him.

IMMUNE SYSTEM SUPPORT

Our immune system is a daily miracle. To supercharge your EMMUNITY, try these tips:

1. **Avoid sugar.** Even a teaspoon of refined sugar can immobilize immune cells for six hours.

2. **Cleanse sinuses.** A simple saline rinse or neti pot (with salt, xylitol, iodine, or colloidal silver) clears bacteria after being in crowds.

3. **Green smoothies & veggie juice.** Carrot and green blends nourish cells and reduce sinus issues.

4. **Sun & fresh air.** *Hashem's* natural vitamin D and oxygen restore energy.

5. **Superfoods.** Ginger, turmeric, garlic, onions, chlorella, spirulina, kefir, sauerkraut, kombucha, fish oil.

6. **Good sleep & rest.** Restoration is sacred.

THOUGHTS

Our thoughts drive our emotions—and emotions determine our health, joy, and connection to *Hashem* and others.

Train your thoughts with meditation, visualization, or EFT tapping. Create a "mastermind" group for encouragement. The mind is the most powerful healing tool *Hashem* gave us.

YOUR BIG "Y"

Each of us is a uniquely Divinely beloved individual—a living representative of the Almighty.

Why does self-care matter? Because the *Torah* says, "*V'chai bahem*"—live through them.

We are meant to live vibrantly, fulfilling our *Torah*-guided purpose.

May we all be blessed to serve *Hashem* with joyful EMMUNITY!

Ita Teigman is a passionate health educator, certified Family Health Coach, and Emett and meditation facilitator for over three decades. She empowers women to take responsibility for their family's physical, emotional, and spiritual well-being through workshops, coaching, and holistic living. Ita also bakes her signature gluten-free Blessed Bagels, promoting health, joy, and Emunah-based living.

✉ **ItaTeigman@gmail.com**

CREATE SELF CARE HABITS

Rejuvenation Rituals:

Practical steps to feel & look amazing this winter

BY YARDENA SLATER

Hello lovely ladies,

I am excited to share with you some of my healthy winter glow up tips!

We tend to eat more heavily and be less active in winter, not to mention the *Chanukah* latkes and *sufganiyot*, all of which tends to throw us off course. Yes, I'm all for having some fun, but we need to be in tip top shape to live life aligned as closely as possible with God, as well as to make it through these exciting yet tumultuous times we are living through.

So, here are some tips from a dedicated Detox Specialist and Face Yoga teacher, to get you back on the healthy self-care path.

1. THE FIRST THING TO DO RIGHT AFTER CHANUKAH IS TO SAY GOODBYE TO ALL SUFGANIYOT, CAKES, COOKIES, ETC.

Processed food is toxic and leads to weight gain, fatigue, brain fog and disease.

Good Bye

2. NEXT, USE THIS RECIPE TO DISSOLVE MUCUS AND AVOID CONGESTION OF ALL SORTS:

22 oz. water (2.75 cups)

2 T. lemon juice, freshly squeezed

2 T. minced ginger

2 T. honey

Shake well and then pour through a fine sieve. You can heat this up or drink it cold. Drink in the morning and throughout the day.

3. CLEANSE YOUR DIGESTIVE TRACT AND MUCH MORE WITH WINTER'S TOP FRUIT—CITRUS!

Citrus is liquid sunlight for the brain. It's an anti-depressant, great for weight loss, for dissolving stagnation in the lymph system and for dissolving hardened masses and tumors in the body. Citrus is an incredible energy producer, and blood cleanser!

Oranges, grapefruits, tangerines, pomelos, lemons and limes. Eat citrus and all fruit on an empty stomach only, so definitely for breakfast and possibly for afternoon snack. The seeds in all citrus fruits are anti parasitic, anti-fungal and anti-bacterial so eat some of the seeds too here and there.

4. CALM AND HEAL YOUR NERVOUS SYSTEM BY TAKING A FEW MINUTES DURING THE DAY TO STOP AND BREATHE.

Deep breathing has been proven to have many benefits mentally and physically.

Here is a quick and incredibly effective breathwork routine:

- ♥ Sit in a comfortable chair.
- ♥ Breathe in through your nose to 100% capacity and exhale through your mouth. 5X.
- ♥ Breathe in through the nose to 100% capacity. Hold for 20 seconds. Exhale.
- ♥ Breathe in through the mouth to 100% capacity and exhale quickly through the mouth. 5X.
- ♥ Breathe in through your mouth to full capacity. Hold for 30 seconds. Exhale.

5. REDUCE FACIAL PUFFINESS AND GIVE YOUR FACE SOME GLOW WITH FACE BRUSHING:

At night, use a dry brush to lightly brush your face in a downward motion. This helps with lymphatic drainage as well as to remove dead skin cells. You can purchase a dry brush on Amazon and at most skincare stores.

6. WANT TO RID YOURSELF OF THAT PESKY DOUBLE CHIN?

Here is a simple face yoga pose to reduce a double chin and tighten the jawline:

- ♥ Sit comfortably and arch your neck back so you are looking at the ceiling.
- ♥ Now stick your tongue out and try touching it as close as possible to your nose.
- ♥ Hold this pose for 20-30 seconds.
- ♥ Now relax. Repeat twice more.

Take a couple of minute breaks to do this 2 or 3 times throughout your day and you will see the difference in just a few short weeks!

7. YOUR MINDSET IS KEY. BECOME AWARE OF YOUR INNER DIALOGUE.

What are you saying to yourself all day long?

Your thoughts and speech have CREATIVE power. They are actually a form of prayer. If your inner dialogue is in contrast with your goals and dreams, shift it to one that is more aligned.

Hashem's infinite love and wisdom are guiding me today.

God is blessing, protecting and expanding all of my work.

I am sending blessings and love to all those whom I am worried about today.

8. FINALLY, GO TO BED BY 10PM.

What's traditionally known as the "beauty sleep", only takes place from the time darkness sets in, until 2am, and you need a minimum of 4 hours per night of this sleep in order to heal, lose weight, and wake up feeling energized & looking younger. So, if the healing hours end at 2am, that means 10pm bedtime max!

Living in alignment with *Hashem* and His laws and principles is the best investment you can make. We are surrounded by an ocean of *Hashem*'s Love. If only we would get rid of even some of the garbage that fills our minds and bodies, we would feel and connect to this Love so much more.

So, let's use the rest of the winter to become a clearer channel for *Hashem*'s light, truth and love!

Yardena Slater is a holistic wellness mentor dedicated to helping women heal naturally, restore vitality, and reconnect to divine balance. She offers private guidance and group programs, including her Winter Beauty Cleanse—a gentle post-*Chanukah* reset designed to rejuvenate body and soul.

- ✉ renewwithyardena@gmail.com
- 🖸 @renew_with_yardena
- 🌐 stan.store/renew_with_yardena

You Are Not Alone: My Journey from Darkness to Courage

BY JESSICA TSUR

*P*anic attacks, daily anxiety, depression, and suicidality.

Illnesses that plague my brain and haunt my life. Diseases that no one can see—that only I can feel. They have robbed me of the ability to stay present, stolen my joy for life, and lied over and over again about who I am and what I can become. They make me feel alone, lost, scared, and hopeless.

Six years ago, after spending my 40th birthday in a psychiatric hospital, I decided vulnerability would be my next step. As a mom of five, a teacher for fifteen years, and the founder of two nonprofit organizations, taking this step was scary. Those who loved me were afraid that if I shared my story, it would affect not only my life but my children's as well. I knew their intentions were to keep me safe—and yet I couldn't handle feeling

Dena Ackerman

alone on this journey. Feeling alone was one of the worst types of pain I have ever experienced. No one spoke about mental health struggles. It was such a taboo subject—one so many wanted to ignore in hopes it would simply disappear.

Luckily, courage won. I started writing and speaking about my mental health challenges—the countless Hatzalah calls when panic told me I was dying, the hopelessness of depression tricking my brain into believing I didn't want to live anymore, the debilitating anxiety and fear around death, the unknowns of medication and the doubt that they would actually work. And guess what? The more I spoke with honesty and truth, the more people reached out—in tears, in pain, in hopes that this new connection with someone who understood would wipe out their loneliness and isolation.

Soon after, my organization CATCH was born—Creating a Team of Courage and Hope.

CATCH focuses on **community, connection, validation, support,** and **camaraderie**—crucial pillars for anyone struggling with their mental health. When I first began CATCH, I was ready to become a *Chai* Lifeline for mental health— ready to build an organization that would provide all the necessary supports for those who struggle and for their families. Slowly, I realized that this dream would take time. I began to understand that each time I shared on various platforms, it always affected at least one person. On some occasions, it even saved lives.

For those who are struggling—or have family members who are—I see you. I understand you. My heart goes out to you. These journeys are incredibly hard to go through alone. CATCH provides weekly community support groups led by professionals. We come together to share our struggles, to offer support and connection, to spend time with others who truly comprehend how hard life can feel sometimes. While we cannot take away each other's pain, we can provide a safe space for vulnerability and truth—a space where those struggling can be seen and heard.

Togetherness is key to healing.

My hope and dream is that all communities will open support groups. You are not alone! We hear those words all the time—but it's up to Jewish communities around the world to show what not being alone truly looks like. The time is now.

Jessica Tsur is a mental health advocate and founder of the non-profit organization CATCH. Drawing from her own struggles with anxiety and depression, she works to destigmatize mental illness and provide a support system for women. Based in Queens, New York, she also founded the local clothing charity, Levli Gemach.

🌐 **Catchsupport.org**
✉ **info@catchsupport.org**
📷 **@catch_support**

From Darkness to Light in Marriage

WITH LAUREN HOFSTATTER, LMHC— THE ORTHODOX THERAPIST

Every marriage faces moments when the light feels dim—when hurt, exhaustion, or distance make love flicker. For Lauren Hofstatter, a wife, mother of ten, and licensed therapist, those moments are not the end but the beginning of healing. With warmth, faith, and candor, she helps couples move from disconnection to reconnection— from falling apart to falling into place.

Finding Hope When Love Feels Dim

Marriage, like the flame of a *menorah*, burns bright when tended—and flickers when ignored. Lauren has spent years sitting with couples at the edge of breaking, where silence or resentment have built invisible walls. "When people reach me, they've usually been holding everything in for a long time," she says. "My first move isn't to fix, but to slow everything down. Decisions made in anger or panic rarely bring peace."

The goal, she explains, is to lower the emotional temperature so both partners can finally be heard. Often, what looks like anger is really pain—the cry of someone who feels unseen.

Trust Can Heal–Slowly

When trust is broken, there is no quick repair. "You rebuild it through micro-moments," Lauren explains. "Keep one promise. Show up when you say you will. Follow through." These small acts form the scaffolding of safety.

She often reminds couples that healing is a process, not a miracle: "Even a shattered bone can become stronger once it heals. Relationships can too—when both people commit to transparency, empathy, and patience."

When Only One Partner Is Ready

Sometimes, only one spouse wants to try. That, she says, is still a place to begin. "About ninety percent of the time, when one person starts growing, the other eventually steps in too," she shares. "Change from one side often sparks curiosity—and hope—in the other."

Lauren's work often starts with the willing partner. When they shift their tone, their patience, or their expectations, the dynamic at home begins to shift as well.

Communication: The Wick of the Flame

"Many couples forget how to talk," she says. "They speak in monologues, not dialogue. They listen in order to reply, not to understand."
 Underneath the anger, she often finds sadness or fear. Her approach teaches couples to strip away defensiveness and speak truth in ways the other can actually hear. "It's not about being right—it's about being real," she adds.

Breaking Old Patterns

Many couples unknowingly "copy-paste" the marriages they grew up watching. "Real change begins when you can gently name those patterns without shaming each other," Lauren explains. "Honesty doesn't have to wound."

She encourages partners to blend empathy with accountability: to set clear boundaries while still assuming the best of each other's intentions.

Respect Across Generations

Words from in-laws or extended family can linger like shadows. "Respect runs both ways," she says. "Talk to your child-in-law with the same courtesy you'd want for your own child. A few thoughtful words—or silences—can protect years of peace."

Rekindling Closeness

Physical and emotional intimacy are intertwined. "If you're not kind outside the home, don't expect warmth inside," she says with a smile. Small gestures—a thank-you, a compliment, a shared cup of tea—can re-ignite the glow that routine often dims. True closeness begins with feeling emotionally safe.

When You Feel Like Roommates

If you're living parallel lives, she suggests starting small:

- Try again. The willingness to try is the first spark.
- Focus on one promise. Reliability rebuilds safety.
- Listen differently. Hear what's under the words.
- Remember your friendship. Marriages rooted in friendship endure.

Dena Ackerman

predicts. The same, she says, is true in marriage. "A single act of empathy, a calm conversation, a sincere apology—each can become the drop of oil that keeps a family glowing through the dark."

She pauses, then adds softly, "Never underestimate the power of small, meaningful steps toward growth. We had a little oil, and it lasted eight days. Sometimes one kind word is enough to start the miracle."

Choosing Your Hard Path

Both paths—staying or separating—are hard. "Many people never stop to ask what they actually need in a relationship," Lauren notes. "Once they do, we can start watering that seed."

Her goal is never divorce—it's clarity. "Staying together just for the kids isn't enough if there's no compassion or respect. But when a couple chooses to work, even after deep hurt, that's where the miracles begin."

A Chanukah Reminder

Chanukah reminds us that one small light can last longer than reason

Lauren Hofstatter, LMHC, is a licensed therapist and faith-based mental health coach helping Orthodox Jews strengthen emotional wellness while staying true to their values. A wife, mother of ten, and active community member, she holds BS and MS degrees in mental health counseling and is certified in DBT and ADHD Clinical Services. She is currently a Clinical Sexology PhD candidate.

🔲 **@theorthodoxtherapist**

🌐 orthodoxtherapist.com

PARENTING
With Intention

BY YACOVA LEIFERT

Dena Ackerman

ILLUSTRATION BY DENA ACKERMAN

As a mother of five and a parenting coach of many, I find toddlerhood to be one of the most magical stages of development. Children begin walking, talking, and exploring their independence while trying to make sense of how they can interact with the world around them. How you support your toddler through this developmental phase can shape the very nature of your entire relationship in parenthood. They are testing boundaries and learning how the world works. It's the first time that they realize they have a will and their own agenda, which may not always align with yours.

Your goal is to encourage independence and cooperation while maintaining boundaries and staying connected by practicing proactive parenting.

Proactive parenting means we need to prepare ahead of time. Kids feel secure when they know what's expected of them. Before going to a restaurant, visiting grandparents, heading to the park, or a playdate, review three simple rules and role-play them at home. Practice them, so when the time comes, you only need a gentle reminder. This is what sets up kids for success.

We show them which behaviors are acceptable and which are not. Most importantly, we do this in a way that is kind and supportive to a toddler's developing mind.

I once heard a parent say, "If I give in, I feel like he runs the show, and if I don't give in, my kid will have a meltdown."

But would it really be so terrible if kids had the occasional meltdown?

Children are born with the full range of emotions—joy, anger, sadness, excitement—but no ability to regulate them. Their feelings come fast and big. I think of it like a baby scorpion: Its sting is stronger, not because it has more venom, but because it hasn't learned to control it. Toddlers are the same. Their "sting" feels intense because they can't yet moderate what's inside.

Kids are allowed to have big feelings about limits while we stay calm and supportive. All feelings are welcome, but all behaviors are not. We are their role models. Children learn from how we show up for them during their big feelings. Not only do they learn by watching how we regulate, but they learn that big feelings are a part of life—my parents are OK with them, I can be OK with them too, until they pass.

Of course, we want our kids to be happy, but life isn't always perfect. Our goal is to build emotional resilience—the ability to feel difficult emotions and still be OK. That's perhaps one of the greatest gifts we can give to our children.

The challenge, however, isn't just what children do—it's what happens inside us when they push back. If their defiance triggers fear or frustration, we may react harshly. Then, both parent and child are in an emotional storm. Nothing good happens there.

Pause. Breathe. Reset.

We need to be the calm in their storm. They aren't giving us a hard time, they are having a hard time. When we shift our perspective, it allows us to show up differently for our children.

One of the most challenging moments is when a child says "No!" We may hear an inner voice whisper, "When I was a kid, I would never have gotten away with that." However, if we want to raise adults who advocate for themselves and voice their opinions, they need to practice. So we teach them how to say "no"…with grace and respect.

When kids are melting down—hitting, screaming, spiraling—it's not time for a life lesson. It's time for support and regulation. Of course, we teach—but later, when they're calm, fed, and open to learning. Then we can say,

"Remember earlier when you were upset?" This is when we can guide them toward better ways to handle it.

Kids don't need to be punished, they need skills to learn how to better handle their feelings, needs, opinions, in more respectful and effective ways.

Parenting isn't about surviving tantrums, it's about shaping relationships. The patterns we build today lay the foundation for trust in the teen years and beyond. We need to show up to parenthood with intention, be proactive, and set healthy boundaries. We do this while we ourselves stay calm and regulated. Like the process of strengthening a muscle, it feels awkward at first, but with practice, it becomes natural. When we parent this way, we're not just surviving parenthood—we're thriving.

Yacova Leifert Originally from Philadelphia, Yacova moved to Israel at the age of nineteen. The proud mother of five children (and, since getting remarried in November 2024, five "bonus children"), she is passionate about empowering parents to raise happy, healthy, and resilient children. Yacova offers personalized parent coaching through her website.

🌐 JoyBasedCoaching.com

Creating Calm: Organizing for Chanukah and the Winter Season

BY CLAIRE BLUMENTHAL-ZEITLER

As the days grow shorter and the air turns crisp, our homes become the center of life. Winter draws us inward, asking us to create warmth, routine, and beauty inside our walls. For Jewish families, *Chanukah* arrives as the season's bright centerpiece: eight nights of light, joy, gathering, and, often, a surprising amount of mess.

This time of year highlights the truth that organization is not merely about having tidy closets or a perfect, Pinterest-ready pantry. It is about creating an environment that supports your family, nurtures your spirit, and allows you to experience the season fully. With a few intentional shifts, your home can accommodate both the glow of *Chanukah* candles and the quiet restfulness of winter.

Make Room for What's Coming

Every holiday brings new things into the home—gifts, toys, Judaica, and the inevitable seasonal gear. Before the first candle is lit, take time to edit what you already own. Donate toys and books that no longer excite your children. Let go of duplicate kitchen gadgets or *menorahs* with missing holders.

This practice is not about scarcity; it's about clearing space so new blessings can be received without becoming overwhelmed. Children especially benefit from seeing that receiving and releasing are two sides of the same rhythm.

45

The Chanukah Station

Few things sap the joy of candle lighting faster than the scramble to find candles, matches, or a tray to protect the windowsill. A dedicated *Chanukah* station eliminates that fluster. Whether it's a tray on a shelf or a basket tucked into a cabinet, gather candles, lighters, foil, dreidels, and chocolate *gelt* in one designated place.

When everything is ready, the ritual feels less like a chore and more like a graceful pause in the evening.

Winter Wear Without the Chaos

The shift in weather brings coats, boots, scarves, and gloves that too easily collapse into a heap by the door. An entryway system—no matter how small—will transform daily comings and goings. Hooks at child-friendly height, bins labeled for each family member, and a mat to catch wet shoes all help maintain order.

When outerwear has a home, the living room no longer bears the brunt of winter's clutter.

Kitchens Built for Frying Season

Latkes and *sufganiyot* are irresistible, but frying has a way of spreading chaos. Before the holiday, pare back your counters so there is actual space to work. Assemble a "frying kit": one heavy pan, a slotted spoon, an oil thermometer, and stacks of paper towels or cooling racks.

You can keep the kit together, ready for its yearly debut. When the oil begins to shimmer, you'll cook with more ease and far less stress.

Curate Cozy Minimalism

With so many hours spent indoors, clutter becomes more visible. Winter is the season to embrace cozy minimalism—keeping only what adds warmth, function, or beauty. Rotate toys so fewer are out at a time. Fold blankets neatly into a basket rather than scattering them across every surface. Choose one or two seasonal decorations instead of crowding shelves.

The result is a home that feels inviting, not overwhelming—a backdrop for meaningful family time and peaceful evenings by the glow of the *menorah*.

Carrying the Light Forward

When the *menorahs* are packed away and the last doughnut has been eaten, the winter stretches on. Use the momentum of *Chanukah* to tackle quiet seasonal projects, such as rotating linens, reviewing pantry staples, or creating a system for winter paperwork.

Organization in this season is not about sterile perfection—it is about creating space for joy. Joy in the nightly rhythm of candles, in the calm of a clear kitchen counter, in the ease of a tidy entryway. By approaching the winter months with intention, you can build a home that reflects both light and serenity.

A Ready-for-Guests Reset

Chanukah is a season of hospitality, from quick candle-lighting visits to evenings of food and laughter. Your home need not be perfect to be welcoming. Adopt the ten-minute reset: sweep everyday clutter into a basket, wipe the counters, and refresh the bathroom hand towel. Small, practiced gestures create an atmosphere that feels prepared, even when guests arrive with little notice.

Claire Blumenthal-Zeitler is the founder of Pemberley Maison, a home organization company under The Pemberley Group. She helps families create calm, functional spaces that reflect both lifestyle and tradition. Claire also designs bespoke dresses through Atelier Blumenthal and runs the Bloomwood Society, a private members' club for women looking to find joy in their lives. She lives in Israel with her family and believes that beauty and order should be a part of everyday life.

🌐 pemberleymaison.com
🌐 bloomwoodsociety.com

Eight Lights
of HEALING

BY BREINDY WARREN LAZOR

W hile each of our holidays has its unique beauty and spark, most of them—let's face it—require a lot of effort and preparation ahead of time. *Chanukah*, on the other hand, is so joyous and carefree, and requires so little work. Everything about this holiday—the bright candles of the *menorah*, the aroma of *latkes* and *sufganiyot*, and the time spent with family and friends—is a welcome reprieve from the dark and cold winter. Which is why it might sound strange, but seventeen years ago, I actually briefly considered skipping *Chanukah* completely.

CANDLE 1 –
THE LIGHT OF LOSS

The backstory is that on the 9th of *Kislev* in 2008, my mother passed away. It was unexpected. It was devastating. The sudden loss threw everything off balance, leaving me feeling as though I were living in an alternate reality. In this new reality, my mother was gone, and it was a long time before I could process the finality of that. The days of *shiva* went by excruciatingly slowly—yet also incredibly quickly. I didn't know it then, but I was just beginning the many stages of grief.

CANDLE 2 – THE LIGHT OF MEMORY

After re-emerging into the world, I was caught off guard one day—shortly after getting up from *shiva*—when I saw *menorahs* and *dreidels* in local shop windows. While time had stopped for me and my family, everything outside our little world had continued. The festive music in neighborhood stores informed me that *Chanukah* was almost here.

I remember walking home that day, feeling a new kind of shock—a shock that time had moved forward and that life around me was continuing.

CANDLE 3 – THE LIGHT OF FAITH

I did a sort of system check. How did I feel about *Chanukah* coming? I decided I didn't feel good about it. It was just over a week away, and thoughts of the warm lights, music, and happiness that I had always associated with *Chanukah* felt impossible to consider. I wasn't ready for any of it.

I couldn't do it, I told myself. Okay, I reasoned, so what then? I tried to imagine skipping it. I would stay in my room while the *menorah* was lit, pretend not to notice it, pretend there was no such thing as *Chanukah*. I would

celebrate it next year. It wasn't too much to ask to play hooky for just one holiday, was it? After all, this was too soon.

I told myself I'd be ready for *Tu B'Shvat*, for *Purim*... In a few months, I could see myself celebrating the *yamim tovim* again. Maybe even *Chanukah*, if it could just be pushed off a bit. But not now. Not this soon.

CANDLE 4 – THE LIGHT OF RESILIENCE

These thoughts tumbled around in my head for a few minutes until they were stopped by a rational voice. It quietly said, "No. That's not how this works. It's *Chanukah* when it's *Chanukah*—and we celebrate it."

And so, I did celebrate *Chanukah* that year. Holding back tears at the *menorah* lighting as I remembered how much my mother loved this *yom tov*; choking on *Ma'oz Tzur* as I heard my mother's voice singing the words; sniffling into my *latkes* as I recalled her cooking them in our kitchen. Somehow, I made it through that first *Chanukah* without her.

CANDLE 5 – THE LIGHT OF GRATITUDE

In the weeks that followed, especially as her *shloshim* approached, I spent more time thinking about what *Chanukah* means to us as Jews—and how everything happens in the right time. *Chanukah* is such a positive, hopeful *chag*, a reminder that *Hashem* is with us in *galus* and that we are never alone as a people. The image I once had of *Chanukah* had been broken. At the time, I might have said it was shattered, but in hindsight, it had simply broken into many big pieces. It was like a puzzle that needed to be put back together—but with one new piece: my mother's death. How could I fit her passing into the framework of this holiday?

CANDLE 6 – THE LIGHT OF RENEWAL

I became determined to find some connection between my mother and the holiday she loved so much. In time, I gradually realized that this was, in fact, a most appropriate time for her passing. She was someone who never felt down for long, who always found a way to bring herself and others out of sadness. She was a problem-solver and an optimist. I imagined my mother looking at us after *shiva* and saying, "Okay, enough of this sadness. *Chanukah* is coming. Go be happy! Live life!"

CANDLE 7 – THE LIGHT OF LEGACY

It was so typical of her to find the light in any darkness. It was truly her nature to always see the good. I came to the conclusion that my mother would have approved of her *yahrzeit* being in *Kislev*, so close to *Chanukah* every year. I found a way to put the pieces back together and fit my mother's passing in—creating a new image of *Chanukah* and *Kislev*.

Each subsequent *Chanukah*, always coming on the heels of her yahrzeit, became slightly easier and increasingly more joyous. Then *Hashem*, in His mercy, added to the puzzle pieces. He granted us a son on the 18th of *Kislev*,

two years after my mother's passing. There were so many miracles and close calls surrounding that pregnancy and birth that I have no doubt my mother was beseeching *Hashem* on our behalf the entire time.

CANDLE 8 – THE LIGHT OF HEALING

A few years later, *Hashem* bestowed upon us a daughter on the 21st of *Cheshvan*, and I was privileged to give her my mother's name. *Baruch Hashem*, my mother's *yahrzeit* is now sandwiched between my children's births—in a manner of comfort that only *Hashem*, in His infinite wisdom, could have arranged.

For me, *Kislev* is filled with contradictions—puzzle pieces that hold both happiness and sadness, darkness and light, death and life. And each year, this amazing, complicated, and wonderful month of *Kislev* culminates in the beautiful holiday of *Chanukah*, when light, hope, and *emunah* triumph over everything.

Breindy Warren Lazor has been an educator for more than two decades, and her writings have been featured in various Jewish publications. She resides in Jacksonville, Florida, with her family.

ONE IN A MILLION:
Vita Goldstein's Life of Miracles

BY VITA GOLDSTEIN

Miracles have a way of quietly shaping a life. Mine began on February 19, 1953, when I was born with a condition that doctors said might not allow me to survive my first year. Against every expectation, I lived, and that first miracle became the foundation for a lifetime of faith, resilience, and gratitude.

I have to say, my mother, Elsie Fetterman, who is 98, healthy, and independent—her strength and perseverance have inspired me from the very beginning.

Vita with her mother Elsie

the trauma of my infant days, I draw strength from knowing I survived for a reason—perhaps to help others, or to pursue my creative passions. Those thoughts inspire me and fill my heart with gratitude. I see *Hashem*'s hand in every step, teaching me that perseverance, faith, and steadfastness can guide us through life's challenges.

Years later, after marrying Reuven in 1976, we faced another test—the long wait to become parents. For five years, we remained childless. I traveled to Yale University Hospital and then to the University of Connecticut Medical Center for tests and treatments. Despite every effort, pregnancy remained elusive. Adoption was suggested, but Reuven and I held onto hope, strengthened by knowing that others around us were struggling, praying, and supporting each other. That connection gave me courage—I never felt truly alone.

In January 1982, I was scheduled for a dye test to check for an obstruction. The appointment was out of town and would require staying over *Shabbat*. Keeping *Shabbat* was deeply important to me, and I worried about how Reuven could stay nearby. Then a hospital clergy stepped in. She arranged a sofa bed for him, so we could be together that weekend without compromising *Shabbat*. Her thoughtfulness brought immense relief and gratitude.

By April, I was pregnant. At first, I didn't believe the home tests—was it really possible? Our daughter was born on December 16, 1982, the seventh night of *Chanukah*. In our home, she became our

From the moment I was born, her courage and intuition were evident. She noticed a red mark on my ear that spread to my cheek immediately after birth. The family doctor dismissed it as a pressure mark. "You're acting like a nervous first-time mother. It will go away," he said. But my mother's instincts would not let her wait. She took me back immediately, trusting her gut even when others doubted her.

Her steadfastness saved my life. When Boston Children's Hospital confirmed I had the largest hemangioma they had ever seen, I was placed on the critical list. Doctors told my parents I might not survive the year. Eleven months later, my brother *David* was born, and miraculously, both children came home safely. My mother often recalls that first miracle as a guiding light in her own life—and mine.

Looking back on that "one in a million" beginning, I feel a deep sense of purpose. While I am separated from personal light—a living reminder of faith, hope, and the rewards of perseverance.

Just a year later, during my second pregnancy, initial testing suggested Spina Bifida. Doctors recommended abortion, warning about the risks and the tight legal window. My gut reaction was simple yet steadfast: "Do you only keep the good ones?" With encouragement from our rabbi, neighbors, and my supportive midwife, Barbara Soderberg, I continued the pregnancy. Further testing revealed the initial result was a false positive, and our second daughter was born healthy, just before Purim in 1984.

Keeping *Shabbat* throughout these medical challenges became my constant spiritual anchor. Even though I did not grow up observing *Shabbat*, I always knew it was something I wanted for my own life—a connection to *Hashem* that could not be broken. No matter what happened in our lives, I always had *Shabbat*, and that unwavering pillar gave me strength in moments of uncertainty.

These experiences taught me lessons that reach far beyond medicine or circumstance. Miracles, I've learned, are not just extraordinary events—they are reminders that faith, hope, and a positive mindset matter. When fear or doubt arises, seeking out supportive friends, family, or professionals, reading uplifting stories, and remembering that *Hashem* is in charge can give the courage to continue. Miracles can happen, and they can bring hope when you feel lost; a quiet message: "You can do it, no matter what."

Looking at my children and grandchildren today, I feel an overwhelming sense of love and gratitude that words cannot fully capture. It is a deep, intangible thankfulness for every breath, every laugh, and every moment together. I am constantly reminded that life, while fragile, is filled with opportunities to witness *Hashem*'s light.

In conclusion: The spirit of the miracles of *Chanukah* are alive and well in our modern world.

Thank you for giving me the honor of writing and expressing our good fortune, and thank *Hashem* for giving me the ability to share this story. My message is simple: 'Think good and it can happen.' It is the positive side of a self-fulfilling prophecy. As the Lubavitcher Rebbe taught: 'Think good and it will be good!'

Vita Goldstein and her husband Reuven made *aliyah* from New Haven, Connecticut, to Rehovot, Israel, in 2010. Vita is an art teacher, calligrapher, and quilter, and enjoys designing her own clothes and sewing quilts for her grandchildren. She is a proud mother of two daughters and grandmother of three, and she is deeply grateful for her family and life in Eretz Yisrael.

IN THE SPACE BETWEEN ASKING AND ANSWERED PRAYERS

BY BARI MITZMANN

It took almost six years between my son and my newest little miracle.

We wanted another child, but it wasn't happening. Month after month, I told myself to have faith, to trust the timing, to let go. But inside, it hurt. There was this quiet, persistent ache that just sat with me, reminding me of what wasn't yet.

During that time, something unexpected happened that, at first, seemed completely unrelated.

An influencer I followed was running a double stroller giveaway. I wasn't trying to win it—I only entered to support the post and tagged friends so they could enter too. I wanted to help her boost it, not win anything.

But I did. I won.

And what should have been a funny, harmless coincidence turned into something else entirely. There were people who were genuinely upset. They commented and messaged saying that I didn't need it, that my kids were already too old for a double stroller. Others said influencers get everything for free anyway, so why should I win?

To be clear, there is no "free." Anything that comes through social media takes work, time, and energy. Sometimes it's hours of content, editing, pitching, and showing up when you don't feel like it. But when people see it from the outside, it looks easy. It looks like it just appears.

I began to feel that this stroller was attracting *ayin hara*, and I didn't want to hold onto something that created such discomfort and negativity. I decided to ask the influencer to choose a single mother to receive the stroller instead. It felt like the right thing to do.

But the truth is, it didn't end there. I felt publicly embarrassed—deeply. The kind of embarrassment that sits in your throat and makes you want to disappear for a while. I cried, and I prayed. I told *Hashem* that if this moment of humiliation had any merit, I wanted to use it for someone else. I prayed that my embarrassment should be a *zechus* for someone very close to me to have a child. Yes, I wanted my own, but in that moment, my heart wanted miracles for her more.

Not long after, something beautiful began to unfold.

People I didn't even know started reaching out. They said they were praying for me. One woman messaged to say her sister was in labor and had added my name to her prayers. The same name that had been in a comment section a week before was suddenly being whispered in a delivery room. It was surreal.

A few weeks later, I went to a Shaindy Plotzker concert that was raising funds for Efrat. I remember walking in feeling fragile, still carrying the weight of the embarrassment and the ache of waiting. During the concert, something happened. There was a small altercation—a moment that caught me off guard and left me shaky and emotional.

Afterward, someone got up and spoke about the organization, about giving, about the value of helping others bring life into the world. Something inside me stirred. I decided, almost impulsively, to donate the amount of the double stroller to Efrat. When I told the founder, I said it half-jokingly but also with a strange certainty: "I'll call you in nine months."

Around the same time, I did a small *segulah* that my friend, Mrs. Shottland, had told me about after she did an *ayin hara* removal for me. Her uncle, a righteous man named **ר׳ יחזקל בן נעימה ורפאל ז״ל**, was known for bringing blessings to those who gave in his merit. I donated two bottles of wine to our *shul* in his name, along with a small candle bearing his name as well.

I don't know which act it was that opened the gates. Maybe all of them together—the giving, the public embarrassment, the prayers, the *ayin hara* removal, the segulah—or maybe none of them in isolation. But something shifted.

It reminded me of another moment years earlier, when I was eighteen years old and in seminary.

That was when I first learned I had PCOS. (Polycystic Ovary Syndrome) The doctor was blunt. He told me it would likely be difficult for me to have children and put me on medication that started to affect my mental health. I felt scared and confused, and I didn't know what to do. My father was close at the time with Rav Nissim Peretz צצ"ל, a Kabbalist in Bnei Brak, so I called him to ask for advice. I told him about the medication and asked whether I should stay on it. He told me to stop and gave me a *bracha* that I should have all my children naturally.

That *bracha* stayed with me for years.

I found out I was pregnant with my daughter a week before I was supposed to start Clomid. My son came soon after—both without any intervention. Two miracles that carried the echo of that blessing.

But still, I wanted more children. And then came the waiting. The years of hoping. The public embarrassment. The giving. The prayers.

And finally, the yes.

He wasn't due until January 20, but our little boy decided to arrive early—

on Shabbos *Chanukah*, 2024. We named him Nissim.

Not just for the miracle that occurred in my body, but for the fulfillment of a blessing spoken over me so many years ago. For the miracle of waiting and still believing. For the miracle that giving, even from a place of pain, creates.

So much of life happens in between the asking and the answer. We don't always know which moment tips the scales—which action, which tear, which choice to give, which moment of surrender. But maybe it isn't about pinpointing it. Maybe it's about doing them all, with a full heart, trusting that *Hashem* knows exactly which piece to use and when.

For me, that's what Nissim represents: The miracle of giving, the miracle of waiting, and the miracle of being seen by the One who never forgets a *tefillah*.

Bari Mitzmann is a social media content creator at @barianna on Instagram and the author of "*Hakol B'Seder:* Finding My Way Back Home." She lives in Nevada with her husband and, *baruch Hashem*, three children.

📷 **@barianna**

THE HOLOCAUST MENORAH

BY MIRIAM RACQUEL (MERYL) FELDMAN

I stood frozen on the threshold of the sunken living room. There before me stood a huge silver menorah, placed prominently on a platform. It felt out of place–almost surreal. This wasn't a Jewish home, but a German-Brazilian mansion nestled in the wealthy suburbs of São Paulo, Brazil.

Little did I know that single moment would alter the course of my life forever.

Just moments earlier, I had been singing the praises of my German-Spanish friend Marina, who had arranged an entire month of exotic travel across Brazil. We had first met at the University of Tübingen, Germany, a year earlier—it was where I had chosen to spend my junior year abroad. Soon after, we had made plans to explore South America together. As a free-spirited Grinnell College grad, my 22-year-old self was pining for adventures.

One of our planned excursions took us to a friend's home on the outskirts of São Paulo. As shanties and makeshift homes gave way to gated mansions and manicured lawns, it felt like crossing from one world into another.

A large fountain and lit-up landscape greeted us upon arriving at the entrance to our destination. We parked the car and knocked on the huge wooden door.

If this was the outside, I wondered what the inside would look like!

The door opened and we were greeted by an elderly gray-haired couple—a short, stout woman and a tall, erect man.

Marina's face lit up, and she grasped the hands of the hostess. "Hallo! I'm Marina and this is my good friend, Meryl."

The hostess put her hand out towards me, "Nice to meet…."

I didn't hear the end of her sentence. My eyes were glued to the *menorah*, and I froze. Why did this German couple have a Jewish article on display in their home?

Wasn't it out of place?

Or was I out of place?

I ignored the hostess's outstretched hand and looked to the man, so straight was his stance, like a soldier. I pointed to the gleaming silver structure and asked clearly in English, "Where did you get that Jewish *menorah*?"

He walked over and stood behind it. With the platform, its largeness reached up to the top of his chest.

His hard German accent sat heavily on the English words he carefully chose, "I'm a collector of things. I brought this with me when I left Germany." The floor dropped out from under me as I nodded and stared. I had no words for his simple explanation, but my mind flooded with Holocaust stories I had heard in high school of Germans ransacking the homes of murdered Jews.

After a long pause, he asked, "Are you Jewish?"

"Yes, my family is Jewish."

A chilled silence filled the room. The quiet spoke volumes.

Lost in my thoughts, I barely heard our hostess's invitation to the table, "Let's sit and eat. The food is getting cold and we want to hear about your travels around Brazil."

Sitting at the table, the couple was the epitome of politeness. I picked at what was on my plate, having left my appetite behind at the doorway to this grand manor. The hosts and Marina babbled in German, and I sat quietly, alone in my thoughts.

As a young woman traveling the world, I hid my Jewish roots, describing myself as an American, never revealing my true heritage. I craved to fit in with the non-Jewish world, having rejected the superficial Judaism from the New York suburbs in which I had been raised. My family had always run from Orthodox Jews who seemed to follow us wherever we moved, from Monsey to Pomona.

What was Judaism anyway? A religion? A culture? A piece of gefilte fish?

But there, standing in this German home, I had felt compelled, from the depths of my soul, to declare my Jewish roots in full force.

This couple had been on one side of the war, my murdered Jewish ancestors on the other. History became present time for me. Was I in the home of a Nazi who had run to South America to escape accountability for his horrible war crimes against the Jewish people? And one who took perverse pleasure in displaying an object that once belonged to a Jew?

When the polite meal ended, I was relieved to escape from this cold place.

Yet, this experience left its mark on my mind, body, and soul. Perhaps it was this acknowledgment of my heritage, born from the crushing magnitude of crimes against my people, that helped propel me into exploring, understanding, and eventually accepting my faith fully.

Chassidus teaches that a Jew is like pure olive oil. The stronger the squeeze, the purer the outcome. Our deepest, everlasting, eternal connection to G-d, connection to our true essence, is revealed in hard times, as we are witnessing today.

In spite of the incredible trials we are facing as a people, as a nation, *Am Yisroel Chai*—the nation of Israel lives— like never before. Stronger, more unified, and more powerful than ever.

May it be *Hashem*'s will that He return all of His children to our promised land, in peace, prosperity, and love, and may He bless the whole world with the coming of *Moshiach tzidkenu.*

Miriam Racquel Feldman transforms women's lives through somatic healing as an award-winning author, dating & marriage coach, and trauma/anxiety specialist. Her innovative somatic approaches have helped thousands heal relationships, resolve trauma, achieve career clarity, and rediscover inner wisdom and joy.

Loved this story? Discover more in her inspiring books— "God Said What?! #MyOrthodoxLife" and "Somatic Healing for the Modest Goddess."

🌐 MiriamRacquel.com

🌐 YourMarriageMagic.com

Finding Miracles in Life

BY SHAINA BINDER

My name is Shaina Binder. I'm 34 years old, originally from Manchester, England, and now live in Ramat Beit Shemesh, Israel. I have three older sisters and am blessed—*baruch Hashem*—to be a wife and mother of two beautiful girls, ages six and four.

As a baby, my parents noticed that I struggled to crawl. Doctors discovered that I had a form of cerebral palsy called CP hemiplegia, which affects the entire right side of my body. The muscles are weaker and can become tight or spastic, especially when concentrating. Because of this, when I learned to write, I used my left hand.

Over the years, I've learned to manage daily tasks—but some things, like carrying groceries or cutting vegetables, remain challenging. Still, I've always focused on what I can do rather than what I can't.

From the time I was little, singing, dancing, and entertaining others filled me with joy. Creating *simcha* and making people happy became my outlet, and I never let my disability define me. My balance was often off, and I would fall, but each time, I got back up with a smile.

Shaina at her graduation

My parents created a warm, safe home where I was encouraged to try even if I failed. That foundation gave me determination and faith. It taught me that we each have a unique mission in this world—one that only we can fulfill.

My greatest joy is living with kindness. Through kindness, we open our eyes to see the daily miracles that G-d gives us—the hidden light that shines through the cracks.

Through every fall, every scar, and every recovery, *Hashem* performed quiet miracles—strengthening my spirit and teaching me to see light in the darkness. That determination made me a fighter. My challenges didn't break me; they built me.

When I was two, another test came my way—alopecia. My mother began finding clumps of hair on my pillow. Alopecia is an autoimmune condition where the immune system attacks hair follicles, leading to hair loss. At first, it was gradual, but by age ten, I had lost all the hair on my head—alopecia totalis. That's when I began wearing wigs.

Throughout my childhood, I went through endless physiotherapy and tried every possible treatment, from herbal remedies to homeopathy. Once, a homeopath even suggested putting frozen peas and hot food on my scalp to "stimulate" hair growth! But over time, I learned that my true healing didn't come from physical remedies—it came from faith, resilience, and love.

The greatest miracle *Hashem* gave me was the ability to bring joy to others.

I was also born three months prematurely, so just being alive and healthy is a miracle.

At sixteen, I had my first surgery on my right ankle to correct my walking pattern. Because of my condition, I used to walk toe-first instead of heel-first. The surgery was successful, though recovery was difficult. I worked with a private physiotherapist who helped me rebuild strength, and a year later, I had a second surgery to straighten my toes.

After both operations, I had to relearn how to walk—and miraculously, one day, I was walking with my mother when my body suddenly remembered how to run. It was as if my brain had been healed.

At eighteen, I made *aliyah* to Israel, knowing deep inside that this was my place. Living here strengthened my emunah in countless ways. When I studied at Bar-Ilan University, walking around the large campus was often exhausting. Yet strangers constantly offered me rides, showing me how *Hashem*'s kindness flows through His people.

Even in recent years, I continue to see small miracles. Once, when my daughter fell asleep in my arms and I had no stroller, a woman I didn't know offered me hers to borrow. It may sound small, but to me, it was *Hashem* whispering, "I see you."

One of the most powerful miracles in my life happened when I was eight months pregnant with my first daughter. While teaching, I slipped and broke my right ankle—the same side affected by my disability. The break was severe, and I needed surgery. *Baruch Hashem*, the baby was completely fine. After months of physio, I regained my strength and walked again.

One *pasuk* that gives me tremendous strength is: "ה׳ לי ולא אירא"—*Hashem* is with me; I will not fear. It reminds me that even when things feel uncertain or painful, *Hashem* is right beside me.

Living with a disability has taught me to embrace vulnerability. When something feels too hard—washing the floor, lifting heavy groceries—I've learned to ask for help. Talking and sharing my story has become a form of healing and self-acceptance.

Two years ago, I dislocated my knee while dancing—twice! This can happen to people with CP because the muscles are weaker. At first, I thought, I may never walk again. But *Hashem* had other plans. With time, patience, and rehabilitation, I recovered fully.

Each of these moments—every surgery, every fall, every act of kindness—has taught me that miracles don't always appear as dramatic events. Often,

they're disguised as small, ordinary moments that remind us we are loved and guided.

My story is one of strength and gratitude. We all have the power to bring more light into the world through empathy and kindness. When we open our hearts, we begin to see the miracles that surround us every day.

This *Chanukah*, may we all strive to light up the world—not only with candles, but with compassion, hope, and faith. Because when we choose kindness, we reveal the light that *Hashem* has placed in each of us.

Shaina Binder, originally from Manchester, England, now lives in Ramat Beit Shemesh. A mother of two, she loves connecting with people and inspiring others. Shaina moved to Israel alone at nineteen after seminary, studied Special Education at Michlalah College, and teaches English to high school boys with love and kindness.

Join her WhatsApp group "ShainaShares" for daily inspiration and motivation from her life.

shainasager@gmail.com

Dear Sister,
Remember Who You Are—
The Shabbos Queen Within You

BY TZIREL LIBA GREENBERG

Every Friday before I light my candles, I slip on a beautiful ring from *Eretz Yisrael* with a *keter* (crown) on it. I put it on to remember who I am: a *bas Melech*, a daughter of the King.

That's what *Shabbos* means to me—remembering who I truly am, even when life feels messy, confusing, or hard.

My journey hasn't been easy. I became frum in my twenties, and like many *baalei teshuva*, I was full of excitement and fire. My family was spiritual but not observant; belief in *Hashem* was real in our home, but *halacha* wasn't part of our lives. When I embraced *Torah*, I thought that was the end of the journey—but it was really just the beginning.

The
Shabbos
Queen Project

Years later, when my children became teenagers, everything shifted. They went through painful struggles, and my own heart broke in ways I never expected. Around that same time, my mother passed away, and my marriage fell apart. It felt like my entire world was falling apart at once. I remember thinking, *Hashem*, what do You want from me? I was drowning.

Then, in the middle of that darkness, I went to a *kinus* with Rav Koledetsky *shlita*. He said, "You don't need more *segulos*. You need *Shabbos*." Then he looked around the room and said, "If you light your candles ten minutes early, you enter the greatest *eis ratzon* in the universe. The heavens open for you."

I wasn't an early-bird type. I had seven kids, a million things to juggle, and I was using every one of those 18 minutes. But I needed salvation, so I tried it. I began lighting earlier. I picked up Rav Pincus's *sefer* on *Shabbos* and discovered that even after 30 years of keeping *Shabbos*, I had barely touched its depth. I started sharing short thoughts with my kids on WhatsApp, then with friends—and slowly those moments grew into what became The *Shabbos* Queen Project.

To me, *Shabbos* is all about remembering our royalty. It's like that scene in The Princess Diaries when the young girl finds out she's actually a princess. Overnight, she has to learn how to walk, talk, and carry herself differently. She realized that with royalty comes great responsibility and great glorious privileges.

When we truly understand *Shabbos*, it transforms the way we live. We realize

we're not just ordinary people rushing through life—we're daughters of the King, preparing to welcome the Queen.

I tell women all the time: you wouldn't show up to meet the Queen of England in your bathrobe—so don't come into *Shabbos* that way either. Get ready, take a deep breath, light with dignity, and let yourself feel the holiness. But being a queen doesn't mean being perfect. It means showing up with grace, no matter how hard life feels. It means carrying yourself with strength, even through tears. That's the beauty of Shabbos—it gives us a chance to realign, to breathe, to remember who we are.

For 13 years, I raised seven children on my own. There were times when I was on the floor crying, saying "thank You, *Hashem*," even when my heart didn't understand. I learned that gratitude isn't just for good days—it's a lifeline when you're in the dark. I said "thank

You" through tears, not because it made sense, but because I needed to hold on to *Hashem*. Over time I realized, I don't have to understand. I just have to trust that He does. Gratitude became my bridge back to light.

If you're going through something difficult, start small. Take five mindful minutes before Shabbos to breathe and connect. Say one *bracha* slowly, with intention. Thank *Hashem* for something tiny. Light doesn't always appear as a big miracle—sometimes it's a whisper, a small flicker that grows when you tend to it.

I often tell women, Shabbos isn't only one day—it's a mindset. Bring it into your Monday. Say "*L'kavod Shabbos Kodesh*" when you cook. Pause before *Kiddush* to feel gratitude. Take a breath before you answer your kids. Use the world around you—the tastes, the smells, the moments—to serve *Hashem* with joy. When you do that, every day becomes a little holier.

There's a teaching that every Friday night, when you say or hear *vayechulu hashomayim* during *kiddush*, first picturing H's creating the world and then with a thought of real *teshuva*, the two angels who accompany you place their hands on your head and grant forgiveness. *Shabbos* is a mini *Yom Kippur*, every single week. It's *Hashem*'s way of saying, Start again, My daughter. You're home.

After remarrying, my husband and I traveled across America in an RV—36,000 miles—singing, speaking, and thanking *Hashem*. We met so many Jews who needed to hear that they, too, are royalty. Some had never lit candles. Some were keeping *Shabbos* halfway. All of them had that same spark. Every Jewish woman has a *Shabbos* Queen inside her. You don't have to be perfect to wear your crown. You just have to remember it's there. Even when life hurts, even when you're tired, even when you feel like you've failed—you're still a queen.

If I could whisper one thing into your heart before this *Shabbos*, it would be this:

You are not alone.
You are not small.
You are not powerless.

You are a daughter of the King.
Light your candles.
Lift your chin.
Straighten your crown.
And remember who you are!

Tzirel Liba Greenberg is a singer-songwriter, speaker, and founder of The *Shabbos* Queen Project, helping women reconnect to faith, peace, and inner royalty through *Shabbos*. A *baalas teshuva* and mother of seven, she and her husband toured America in an RV, sharing music and *emunah*. Book her for a concert or speaking event.

Instagram & Podcast:
@shabbosqueenproject

theshabbosqueenproject@gmail.com

The Humans of Hanukkah

BY CHAYA LESTER

Chanukkah is a celebration of miracles. For me, I zip-line along the continuum of the miraculous and the mundane. Some moments, I'm the confident embodiment of the fact that God is running the show—the One who pays my bills and rough drafts my scripts. The One who masterminds all of this magnificence.

And then there are the equally convincing moments of crashing into a material world gone so very wrong—an authorless narrative where all that's certain is death and taxes.

And then there's *Chanukkah*.
In *Yerushalayim*. Nachlaot, to be precise. There's the dramatic amble down my alleyway lit up by flames. There's the nightly spiritual block party right outside my door, and once again I'm utterly floored by the miracles that house my days.

We have been brought home. And it wasn't a given either. It was a highly unlikely, couldn't-have-dreamed-of-how-good-it-could-be kind of thing. And it happened—to me, and to a whole unlikely slew of us too. Brought home from the farthest reaches of *galut* and cluelessness to take root. To take old family trees and f-i-n-a-l-l-y replant them in the soil of our souls. Every inch and inkling of our Israel reality is a miracle—pure and simple—and yet so hard to articulate with its deserved grace.

But at least I can try, with a few wordy snapshots of *Chanukkah* here in my hood. I pray a glimmer can shimmer forth that expresses this miraculous reality. So here we go—step out the door and onto the street. Welcome to *Nachlaot*, the beaming, forever-scheming-for-meaning heart of Jerusalem.

TAKE IT TO THE STREETS

Mine is a thin-limbed alleyway sculpted with 150-year-old Jerusalem stone. It's dark—except for these little metal and glass houses of candles every dozen paces or so. Around here, you don't just light candles in windows and leave it at that. You go out of your way to bring the flames into the streets. The most devoted homes have outdoor display cases built just for these eight days of the year.

OILS WELL THAT ENDS WELL

I grew up impeccably assimilated in Memphis, Tennessee. My favorite *Chanukkah* ritual was driving around looking at Christmas lights, high on sugar and *Chanukkah* gelt. I still get nostalgic for all that sparkle and glow. And yet, these humble flames put all that electricity to shame. As far as the soul is concerned, a thousand reams of electrical lights can't beat the soft timbre of these oil-based flickers.

Now, I do like to wax nostalgic, but it's not wax that anoints the Messianic moments—it's oil, my friends. And we've got it flowing with abundance down the Nachlaot streets.

MAKE SURE TO MAKE MUSIC

A half-block away marks the arrival at the Be'er Sheva Street Light Show featuring the Hullman Family Band. Every year Rabbi Barak pulls out his life-size *chanukkiyah* with enough oil to last till morning. For hours, he strums his guitar and lights up tune after tune—with all seven of his children to boot. There's a basket of instruments at his feet for all who pass by to join in the jubilee.

THE GOLDEN RULE–
MEET THE NEIGHBORS

By this point, it's already a party. There are families, couples, singles—but the golden rule on *Chanukkah* is that everybody mingles. When we first moved in, we hadn't even met our next-door neighbors—until *Chanukkah* hit and there we all were, lighting our candles together on the street. We bonded over a roaring round of *Ma'oz*

Tzur and a few *l'chaims*. Boom—lifelong friends. Communing with community is just an undeniably holy thing.

REMEMBER:
WE ARE THE MIRACLES

On *Chanukkah*, we aren't just witnessing miracles. We are the miracles. The humans of *Chanukkah*. We are all zip-lining between the celestial and the mundane. The two opposites meet and mix in us—just like the darkness and the light, the hidden and the revealed.

All in all, it's all in here. So, Happy Lights from Jerusalem's Hub of the Holy.

Chaya Lester is a seasoned psychotherapist, Jewish educator, and spiritual guide. She co-directs Jerusalem's Shalev Center for Jewish Personal Growth, synthesizing the best of Jewish wisdom and psychological healing. In addition to her M.A. in Clinical Psychology, Chaya did extensive doctoral work at Oxford University. She regularly leads spiritual journeys and retreats throughout Israel and worldwide.

If you enjoyed this article, discover more in her book "Lit: Poems to Ignite Your Jewish Holidays," available on Amazon.

🌐 chayalester.com

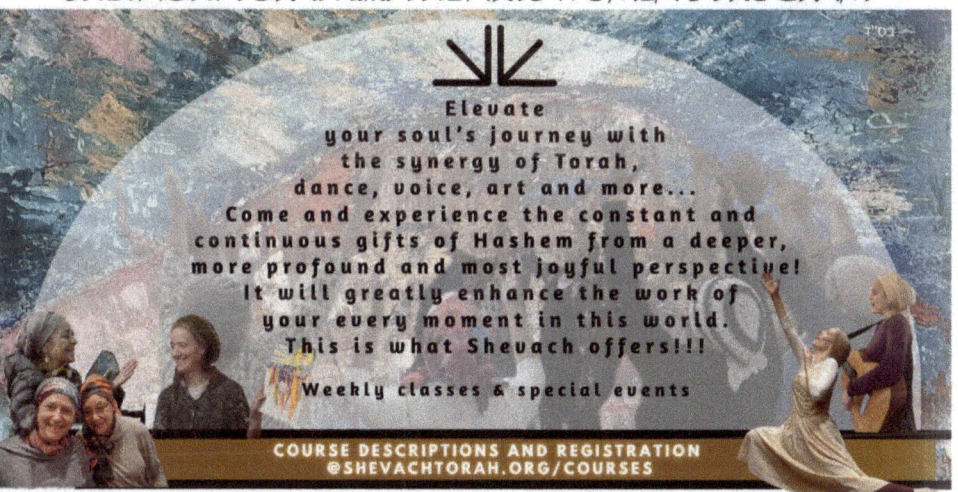

Women at the Heart of the Chanukah Miracle

BY TANYA GARBER

Candles possess something very special that makes them more spiritual than physical. When we draw on physical resources, they become diminished, yet spirituality expands and grows as it is used.

Consider time and money—when spent, they decrease. Food used from the fridge leaves shelves depleted. Even modern energy sources, like electric cars or mobile phones, need to be recharged. But spiritual matters increase as we share them.

When I use my skills and knowledge to teach, the student learns—and I grow in experience, understanding, and wisdom. Sharing love with others engenders more love, not less. Spiritual gifts result in gain for both giver and receiver.

Candles share this spiritual property. When one candle lights another, the original flame remains bright. Its light is not diminished by being shared—on the contrary, both flames together create greater brightness.

The Miracle of the Oil

The *Gemara* in *Shabbos* (21b) describes how, after cleansing and purifying the *Beis Hamikdash* from the defilement of the Greeks, the *Kohanim* sought to light the *Menorah*. Only one small jar of pure, sealed oil could be found—enough to last just one day. Miraculously, it lasted for eight days, long enough to produce new pure oil.

Interestingly, there is no mention of this miracle in *Al HaNissim*. Instead, that prayer focuses on the military victory of the few Kohanim over the mighty Greek army. Why is this historical miracle emphasized, while the oil—ostensibly the reason for the festival—is omitted?

Many daily miracles occurred in the *Beis Hamikdash*—what, then, was so unique about this one?

Oil and Its Symbolism

In *Halacha*, there are seven substances defined as "official liquids," remembered by the Hebrew acronym *Ya"d Shacha"t Da"m* (י״ד שח״ט ד״ם): *Yayin* (wine), *Dam* (blood), *Shemen* (oil), *Chalav* (milk), *Tal* (dew), *Dvash* (honey), and *Mayim* (water).

Each liquid corresponds to one of the seven major Jewish festivals:

Purim	wine
Pesach	blood
Shavuos	milk
Rosh Hashanah	honey
Yom Kippur	dew
Sukkos	water
Chanukah	oil

Oil has two notable properties:
It does not mix with other liquids; it remains distinct and separate.
It rises to the top—it floats above other substances.

This mirrors the Jewish people. The Greek (Yavani) goal was not exile or destruction, but assimilation. They wanted to blur distinctions—to make the *Beis Hamikdash* and the Jewish people ordinary. They sought to "spoil our oil" and make it *tamei*, impure.

But just as oil rises, the Jewish nation remains distinct—*kadosh*, set apart for holiness.

The Women of Chanukah

The *Gemara* in *Shabbos* (23a) teaches that women are obligated in the *mitzvah* of ner *Chanukah*, since they were also involved in the miracle. The Rashbam explains that women were not merely involved—they were central.

Usually, women are exempt from time-bound *mitzvot*, but *Chanukah* is an exception. Though married women generally do not light the *chanukiah* (as their husbands fulfill the *mitzvah* for the household), they are deeply connected to its light.

Women traditionally refrain from doing work for half an hour after lighting, signifying a spiritual *Yom Tov* unique to them. This custom reinforces their pivotal role in the *Chanukah* miracle.

Heroines of the Miracle

Chanah, The Daughter of Matisyahu HaKohen Gadol: The Greeks enacted a cruel decree that every bride must first be defiled by a Greek general. In protest, Jewish families avoided public weddings. At one wedding, Matisyahu's daughter publicly tore her garment, shaming her brothers into action. She reminded them of Shimon and Levi, who defended Dinah's honor. Her courage sparked the Maccabean revolt.

Yehudis bas Yochanan: Yehudis, using her wit and bravery, fed the Greek general Holofernes salty cheese, gave him wine, and beheaded him in his drunken sleep. Her act led to panic among the enemy and victory for her people.

Because of Yehudis's deed, it became customary to eat dairy foods on Chanukah. Women's refraining from work after candle-lighting also commemorates their role as active participants in the miracle.

Appreciating Miracles

Why was the miracle of the oil chosen as the defining feature of Chanukah, rather than the military victory?

The victory was essential—it ensured our survival. But the oil miracle was superfluous. It demonstrated *Hashem's* love, not merely His providence. He gave us a miracle that we didn't need, simply to show that His care extends beyond necessity—it is personal and affectionate.

That is why *Al HaNissim* focuses on the war: it expresses gratitude. The oil miracle expresses relationship. Both are vital—one reminds us to thank, the other to love.

The Name and the Meaning

The word *Chanukah* derives from חנוכה—dedication—marking the rededication of the *Beis Hamikdash*. It is also read as ונח ה״כב—"they rested on the 25th," for on the 25th of *Kislev* the Jewish people rested from battle.

> *Chanukah* celebrates not only victory but peace, the ability to once again light the Menorah and feel *Hashem's* loving embrace.

The Shamash in Our Lives

The *shamash* candle, used to light the others, remains burning even after its work is done. It stands ready to rekindle another flame if needed.

We, too, can be *shamashim*—kindling light in others. Parents, grandparents, teachers, rabbis, rebbetzins, mentors—all serve as guiding flames, illuminating paths for those around them.

This *Chanukah*, as we light our *chanukiah*, let us also brighten the lives of others—sharing warmth, kindness, and light that never diminishes.

Tanya Garber has been a community *rebbetzin* for over 18 years and lives in Edgware, London, with her family. She works as a specialist women's health radiographer at the Wellington Hospital in London, teaches *giyores* students for the London Beth Din, and gives *shiurim* in her community. Her favourite *mitzvot* are *hafrashas challah* and *hachnasas orchim*. She enjoys swimming, ceramics, calligraphy, and painting.

✉ **Tgarber613@gmail.com**

Interview with Rabbanit Yemima Mizrachi:

"We Are the Generation with the Yam Suf Opening Before Our Eyes"

BY SAMANTHA LEVY

Meeting Rabbanit Yemima Mizrachi in Jerusalem was deeply inspiring. Her weekly Tuesday night *shiur* at the "Rabbi Meir Baal HaNes" Synagogue (7 Hagar St.) draws women from all walks of life. Known as one of Israel's most influential women and among the most sought-after speakers today, she stays long after her class, as a line of women patiently waits to receive her *bracha*. She looks into each woman's eyes with heartfelt *kavanah*, blessing with love and strength. In this interview, the Rabbanit shares her reflections on *Chanukah, emunah*, and the miracles unfolding in our time.

What closure message do you have for us on the topic of the war, the hostages, and all that we've gone through up until now?

So, a closure... I don't think we can already talk about a closure. But I see huge *nissim*, and I see huge *nashim*. I see women with mental and physical strength—women who have to care for their children while their husbands are at war—and the mental power of holding on, *davening*, and doing *chesed*.

The closure is not here yet—but the opening of the great *Geulah* has begun. I think we are the generation with the Yam Suf being opened, mamash (truly) before our eyes.

What do most people not know about *Chanukah* symbols such as the *sevivon*, *Chanukah gelt*, and others?

I think the message of *Chanukah* is that so many times you hear about *segulot*—to *daven* near the *chanukiah*, to put a small *petek* (note) and ask for something—and you've done so many things, yet it didn't help. So why stand again and wait for the light?

Then comes the *chanukiah* and says: it accumulates. The first candle joins the second, and the third joins the second and the first.

All your efforts are being counted. *Hashem* sees them all. You do not light the eighth candle by itself—it has its special light because of the seven hard years you had before. The light is made from your small deeds and your small efforts. And all those *segulot* you placed your *emunah* in—they are never in vain.

It's never in vain. Never.

Do you have a personal miracle or *Chanukah* story that has touched your life?

Yes, I do. I had a son—his name was *Yosef Chaim*. He was very, very sick. His heart was weak, and once he suffered a severe heart attack. Afterwards, the doctors called me in and said, "He cannot see. He's become blind."

I watched as they shone light before his eyes, and nothing changed. My heart broke. I knew he wouldn't live long, but at least I had hoped he could still see his brothers, his sisters, and his *ima*.

Then, one evening, I stood before the *Chanukah* candles, and suddenly—I was sure I must be imagining—but I saw the *ishon*, the tiny pupil of his eye, growing and shrinking in the candlelight. And there it was—moving again.

I cried out, "Hey, *ma zeh*?!" (What is this?!) I ran to bring him to the doctor, and he said, "He really sees again!" *Baruch Hashem*. The cells of his brain had renewed themselves. From then on, *Yosef Chaim* could see us until his last days. I'll never forget it.

For those who feel down, disconnected from *Hashem*, or really weak in *emunah*, what message would you give them for *Chanukah*?

I saw it from the war we've all gone through. When someone tells me,

"Ein li emunah—I don't have faith," I understand her, and I believe her.

But when she says, *"Ein bi emunah*—I don't have faith inside myself," I do not believe her.

The Rebbe of Slonim, the *Netivot Shalom*, Rabbi *Shalom* Noach Berezovsky, used to say: *"Yehudi chayav leha'amin shehu ma'amin."* A Jew must believe that he believes.

You have to believe that you believe— that you have *emunah* inside you.

And we saw it with our hostages—they didn't know they had *emunah*. If you had asked them before, they would have said, "Ein li *emunah* ba'*Hashem*." But they did. And that's what we all discovered.

You are a symbol of elegance, beautiful *avodat Hashem*, and devotion to family and community. What is your advice on how we can ignite our inner light—and the light of others— no matter how busy we are?

Wow. Thank you. I think the answer is: look at someone's face.

So many times, you can think of someone or something—but when you look at her face or his face, everything changes. I always say: look at one another. Truly meet one another.

Only when you look at someone's face can you realize how much you don't know them. He can be a *smolani* (left-wing), and he can think the opposite of you—but when you look at him, you

75

suddenly understand, "Hey, I don't know him at all."

Meet one another in order not to know— to know how much you don't know.

It's the *Parashat Vayigash* we read on *Chanukah*—the story of *Yosef HaTzadik*

and his brothers. You thought you knew this boy. He was always teasing you. You hated him. But when you look at his face, you understand—we never really knew who he was.

So look at someone's face—only to know that you do not know them at all.

Rabbanit Yemima Mizrachi was born in Casablanca, Morocco, to Rabbi Elinatan and Tirtza Rothschild. She was named in connection with the Six Day War, shortly before her birth. Raised in Jerusalem, she trained as a lawyer before becoming one of Israel's most beloved *Torah* teachers. Together with her husband, Rabbi Haim Mizrachi, she co-founded the Avney Kodesh Yeshiva, dedicated to inspiring and guiding Jewish youth.

Known for her warmth, humor, and deep wisdom, Rabbanit Yemima inspires thousands worldwide through her weekly classes, bestselling books such as Parsha Ve'Isha, and her radio programs on Kan Moreshet, Kol Barama, and *Kol Chai*. Her teachings bring *Torah* to life through a uniquely feminine and joyful lens—empowering women and conveying a message of faith, connection, and sisterhood. She also serves as President of the CER *Rebbetzin* Training Programme.

🌐 **Parasha.org**

Samantha Levy is a digital marketing expert and educator helping Jewish and Israel-oriented organizations reach their audiences through strategy, storytelling, and social media. With experience in leadership, diplomacy, and public speaking, she combines purpose with professionalism to advance Jewish history and visibility online.

Connect on Instagram
📷 **@samanthalevy**

Learning to Shine Your Light

BY JORDANA (BARUCHOV) GREENFIELD

There's something quietly powerful about a small flame. It doesn't roar or demand attention. It simply shines; steady, warm, and sure of itself. And in that steady glow, it does something remarkable: it transforms darkness into light.

Every year, as *Chanukah* arrives, our homes fill with that familiar golden shimmer; one tiny flame on the first night, two on the next, until our windows and doorways glow with dancing light. But *Chanukah* isn't just about lighting candles; it's about learning to live as one.

ART BY SEFIRA LIGHSTONE

Light as a Declaration

Most Jewish rituals are private; between us and God, between the heart and heaven. But the *mitzvah* of the *Chanukah menorah* is different. We are told to place it in the window or by the doorway, for the world to see. The purpose is not just to remember the miracle, but to publicize it; to let our light spill beyond the safety of our walls.

In Hebrew, the word for "miracle" is *nes*. But *nes* also means a "banner" or "flag"; something lifted high for all to see. When the *Torah* describes *Moshe* raising the copper serpent on a *nes*, it wasn't just an object; it was a symbol, a message of hope and healing, visible to everyone.

So too, the lights of *Chanukah* are our nes: our banner. They declare who we are and what we stand for; that even in darkness, we believe in light. That even when faith feels fragile, we still kindle the flame.

Miracle = Rising After the Fall

Hidden in the word *nes* itself is a secret. The Hebrew letters נ (nun) and ס (*samech*) tell a story. Nun comes from *nofel*: to fall. *Samech* comes from *somech*: to support, to lift up. A *nes*—a miracle—happens when something that has fallen finds the strength to rise again.

Chanukah, at its core, is not about the oil that burned for eight nights. It's about the people who refused to let their light go out. The Maccabees weren't superheroes. They were regular people who faced overwhelming odds and chose to believe that their spark mattered. They fell, and rose again. And through that courage, they created the space for miracles to happen.

Becoming a Living Menorah

We often imagine miracles as flashes of divine intervention; dramatic, rare, reserved for biblical times. But what if the true miracle is quieter? What if it's the moment we choose faith over fear, kindness over cynicism, light over despair?

Every time you rise after disappointment, every time you hold onto hope when things feel uncertain, every time you choose love when it would be easier to turn away; that is your *nes*. You become a living *menorah*.

Just as the *menorah* must be placed at the edge of our homes; between the private and the public, our own light, too, is meant to shine beyond ourselves. We are not meant to keep our strength, our faith, or our joy hidden inside. The world needs to see it. You never know who is watching from the dark, waiting for a reason to believe again.

Owning Your Light

It's not always easy to shine. We live in a world where confidence is often mistaken for arrogance, and where women especially are taught to dim their brilliance so others feel comfortable. But the *menorah* reminds us: light does not compete. It multiplies. When you light your candle from another, the first doesn't lose its flame; it gains company.

Your light was never meant to be hidden or compared. It was meant to inspire. To remind others that they have light, too. Maybe your light is the way you listen. The laughter you bring into a room. The honesty that makes people feel safe. The resilience that comes from all the times you've fallen and gotten back up again. Whatever your light looks like, it's needed. It's holy.

The Window Test

Here's a thought experiment: if your inner light—your kindness, your courage, your faith—were placed in a window for the world to see, what would it look like? Would it flicker with doubt or stand tall with quiet confidence? Would it burn out when challenged or glow brighter when the wind blows?

The placement of the *menorah* teaches us something profound. The goal isn't to hide from darkness but to meet it, face-to-face. To say, "I see you; but I also see the light within me."

Darkness doesn't disappear when light enters. It transforms. And maybe that's the lesson of *Chanukah*: not to wait for perfect conditions before shining, but to shine because the night is dark.

Shining Together

When we light our menorahs, we're not just reenacting an ancient miracle; we're continuing it. The same light that glowed in the Temple thousands of years ago still flickers in our homes, our hearts, our stories. It connects generations; from the Maccabees' courage to our own small acts of faith.

And when you place your *menorah* in your window this year, remember; you are part of that chain of light. Your flame joins countless others, across time and space, all declaring the same simple truth: the light of the Jewish spirit never goes out.

The Call of the Season

This *Chanukah*, don't be afraid to take up your place by the window. To live like a *nes*; a walking banner of light and hope. To share your warmth, your joy, your resilience with those around you. To shine not because everything is perfect, but because you've learned that light is born in the struggle.

You don't need to be extraordinary to bring light into the world. You just need to be willing to burn brightly; right where you are.

So go ahead. Light your candles. Place them where the world can see. And remember—every small flame, including yours, has the power to turn darkness into day.

Jordana (Baruchov) Greenfield is a Soul Coach, *Torah* Influencer, and host of the Drink It In podcast. Known as @Drinkitin_Jordana, she serves as Director of Social Media and Marketing Strategy for Renewal and inspires thousands through her podcast, social media, and speaking. A devoted mother of six and a proud grandmother, Jordana uplifts hearts with warmth, wisdom, and authenticity.

✉ jbaruchov@gmail.com

THE BEAT OF A BUSY SOUL:
JUDITH GERZI

ON THE LIGHT, THE LESSONS, & THE MUSIC OF LIFE

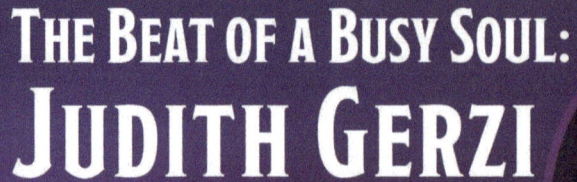

PHOTO BY YAACOV GERZI

INTERVIEW BY ANNIE ORENSTEIN

One of the very first performers I worked with when I started out producing shows for women in the arts was Judith. Judith's soulful music brings women together in a new way. After hearing Judith's incredible voice, I knew Jewish women needed to hear her and be inspired. Over the years, I have had the privilege to provide open mics so that Judith and other women can gain valuable stage experience to go out into the world with their own voice, touching the hearts of women around the world. I also had the privilege to help Judith publish her first album Awakening. What a beautiful journey to be a part of!

YOUR SONGS BLEND SOUL, JAZZ, AND SPIRITUALITY. WHERE DO YOU DRAW INSPIRATION FROM WHEN YOU WRITE OR PERFORM?

I always longed to sing, but I was painfully self-conscious and had very low self-esteem. I also didn't think there was space in the *frum* world for someone like me to perform. Growing up, I'd occasionally come out of my shell singing with my guitar, but I never imagined this could really be part of my life.

Everything changed when my holy husband encouraged me to perform a small concert in Hebrew, for a group of Israelis. Afterward, a woman came up to me in tears and said it was the first time she truly felt someone meant every word they sang—and that through

PHOTO BY YAACOV GERZI

that moment, she started to connect to *Hashem*. It was a moment of awakening. I realized that music could reach people's souls in ways nothing else could.

After that, I sang in a women's competition called Wanna Be a Star that you, Annie, produced. At first, I'd been worrying about how I was being perceived rather than what I was giving. Once I understood that, I started to perform from a place of giving rather than fear.

HAVING A GIFT ISN'T ABOUT YOU; IT'S ABOUT WHAT YOU DO WITH IT.

In the beginning, I wasn't yet writing my own songs—I used familiar melodies and infused them with meaning. Only later, after a personal trauma, I began writing. My first original piece, *Hushaby*, came from deep gratitude after challenges with fertility. Over the years, both joy and pain have shaped my music and my outlook on life. They taught me to be thankful even when

things aren't easy, because those moments often push us higher. That's what my music is about—finding the light within the struggle.

"BURN BRIGHT" IS SUCH A POWERFUL TITLE. WHAT WOULD YOU TELL A WOMAN WHO FEELS SHE'S LOST HER SPARK AND WANTS TO "BURN BRIGHT" AGAIN?

Burn Bright is about celebrating light, remembering miracles, and standing strong even when people try to dim our glow. The message is that the Jewish people have always endured—and we will continue to shine. It's about hope, strength, and trusting that *Hashem* is with us through every challenge, lighting our path forward.

WHAT DO YOU HOPE WOMEN FEEL WHEN THEY LISTEN TO YOUR MUSIC?

I want Jewish music to be professional, soulful, and something you listen to because you love it—not just because it's "kosher." I strive for my music to feel real, authentic, and emotionally resonant.

People often tell me they didn't know this kind of soulful Jewish music existed— that it touched them and inspired hope, self-belief, and connection to *Hashem*. One time, a mother and daughter came to me crying. The girl said she hadn't believed she could keep *kol isha* and still sing meaningfully. She saw the *kedusha* in it and realized that, if I could sing for women and reach hearts, she could too!

MANY OF YOUR SONGS CARRY THEMES OF LIGHT, HEALING, AND RETURNING TO HASHEM. WHAT PERSONAL EXPERIENCES SHAPED THOSE MESSAGES?

I've faced several serious health challenges over the years, though you might not see it from the outside. Those experiences taught me resilience, gratitude, and the beauty of raw honesty. Even the most painful moments can be *Hashem*'s way of helping us grow. If we are lucky, we get to glimpse why we needed to go through certain things.

WHAT'S NEXT FOR YOU—ANY NEW PROJECTS, ALBUMS, OR COLLABORATIONS?

I'm working on new music that feels even more "me." Some songs come from childhood memories and experiences I've carried for years. One project close to my heart deals with bullying—something I've experienced and helped others through.

There are some exciting collaborations ahead and I'm revisiting older pieces, re-arranging and bringing them to life, *b'ezrat Hashem*.

I feel incredibly blessed to be performing internationally, both in *Eretz Yisrael* and abroad, thanks to my dear friend *Bracha* Jaffe and AHAVA, who helped connect me with students and opportunities overseas.

Above all, my family comes first. My husband and children are the heart of everything I do. I love taking them with me when I perform, and my girls and I are at the start of something special, *iy"h*.

Rebbetzin Judith Gerzi is a singer-songwriter and international performer based in Ramat Beit Shemesh. She teaches voice at the Ramat Beit Shemesh Dance & Music Academy, in seminaries across Israel, and offers private one-on-one vocal coaching. Together with her husband, Rabbi Yehoshua Gerzi, the rav of their community, she leads inspiring workshops that blend music, *Torah*, and personal growth. They are blessed with a large, beautiful family.

✉ Ygerzimusic@gmail.com
📷 @judithgerzimusic

Annie Orenstein, has been producing shows for women and girls since 2006. In 2010, she co-founded Spotlight On Women. She is passionate about producing open mics for performers to grow professionally and for Jewish women to be inspired. She also hosted Spotlight On Women Radio, and writes in local newspapers and magazines highlighting artists. She lives in Maaleh Adumim with her family.

✉ Annie.spotlight@gmail.com

A Symphony of Teshuva: Inside the Zmora Women's Orchestra

BY CHAVA RACHEL SABAN

SPOTLIGHTING THE ARTISTRY AND INSPIRATION OF

BRACHA BDIL

There are moments in life when the melodies we thought we had forgotten suddenly resurface, carrying us home. My own journey as a violinist has circled from the bright lights of the San Francisco Youth Symphony to the soulful glow of Jerusalem's Zmora Women's Orchestra, where I now play under the baton of the remarkable composer and conductor Bracha Bdil.

Meeting Bracha was like finding the missing instrument in an orchestra I hadn't realized was incomplete. Her passion for both classical excellence and *Torah* values infuses Zmora with purpose: here, music is not performance for its own sake but an *avodat Hashem*—sacred service. As a fellow musician and ba'alat *teshuva*, I wanted to understand how she bridges two spheres that often seem worlds apart: music as a profession and religion.

A COMPOSER'S CALLING

"When I was ten," Bracha begins, "I studied organ privately. Later I wanted piano, but my mother said, 'We already have three organs!' So I learned accordion instead. Eventually, I saved up for secret piano lessons at a neighbor's house until my mother agreed to bring a piano home."

Looking back, Bracha now sees how playing organ planted the seeds of composition—layering voices, exploring sound textures, and improvising. "I discovered my own melodies before I even knew what composing was," she says. After seminary, where she studied music education, she pursued degrees in voice and piano at the Levinsky College through Ron Shulamit Conservatory and later, a 1st and 2nd degree in music composition at the Jerusalem Academy. "When I began to understand the principles of harmony, I realized: if Mozart could do this, so can I! Maybe it was ego—but a healthy ego. As it is said, 'Envy of scribes increases wisdom.'" (Pirkei Avot 4:21)

FAITH IN SOUND

When I ask Bracha about obstacles as a *Torah*-observant female composer, she laughs. "Obstacles? None! These days, commissioners want under-represented voices—women even have an advantage."

Women coming to a Zmora concert experience much more than passive listening to beautiful music. Before each piece, Bracha shares short explanations linking some aspects of the music to our lives as Jewish women. At our last concert she likened a repeating Bach motif to our persistent tefillah to save *Am Yisrael* from so much suffering. Hearing that changed the piece for me forever"Music is an abstract art, which is why it fits so beautifully for religious women. Because it's mostly non-verbal, it becomes a vessel for spiritual meaning. At each concert, I choose to interpret the music in the spirit of the times or in connection with the upcoming holiday. And this is one of the reasons that after the shock of the outbreak of the 7/10 war, and the postponement of the concerts- we chose to continue holding them. Thus,

PHOTO COURTESY OF M BDIL

easy to get to the hall, but my mother insisted that we hear live classical music. If a woman brings her daughter or granddaughter to a concert, and together they experience the beauty of live classical music—maybe that spark will ignite a lifelong love. That's how we build appreciation, one heart at a time."

THE VIOLINIST'S RETURN

My own musical journey began when my mother noticed me singing Beatles songs in perfect pitch during car trips. At the age of 4, I was a Suzuki violinist; by high school, performing Beethoven symphonies with the San Francisco Youth Symphony on the grand stage of Davies Hall. Tears would stream down my face as the music swelled—it felt like prayer.

Yet behind that beauty, I glimpsed a darker score: fierce competition, inappropriate relationships, and spiritual emptiness. When I later came to Israel and embraced *Torah*, I thought I had to choose. I packed away Bach and Tchaikovsky, deeming classical music too secular. Years passed until my daughters began learning strings, and through them, classical music re-entered my home.

Then one day, in Uman, as I was playing by Rebbe Nachman's *tziyun*, a girl approached me: "You should play with Zmora." A professional frum women's

we declared our affirmation of life, proving that death cannot weaken the human spirit."

THE CONDUCTOR'S BATON

Bracha assumed leadership of Zmora in 2018, succeeding founder Rina Shaeffer. "I had conducted choirs and taken a few conducting classes," she explains, "but when the opportunity came, I just jumped into the water."

For Bracha, Zmora is more than an ensemble; it is a mission. "I remember my mother taking me and my sister- when I was seven or eight- on a stormy, rainy night to hear the Zmora orchestra conducted by Rina Shaeffer. It wasn't orchestra in Jerusalem? It sounded too good to be true—until I joined my first rehearsal and felt healing wash over me. No competition, only camaraderie. These women applauded each other's solos with genuine joy. What a miracle!

ESHET CHAYIL—THE SONG OF JEWISH WOMEN

This past year, Zmora premiered Bracha's "Eshet Chayil" choral symphony, each movement dedicated to a different biblical heroine—Miriam, Ruth, Esther, and Yehudit—performed with three girls' choirs and soloists in period costume. The work pulsed with suspense, drama, and holiness.

"I write a lot from Jewish sources," Bracha explains. "It's part of who I am. During these times, hearing about women in captivity who still cared for others inspired me deeply. Throughout our history, Jewish women have shown extraordinary courage. I wanted to commemorate their spiritual strength through music."

KIBBUTZ GALUYOT, AND MIRACLES

Driving home from rehearsal, singing the music we practiced for the past few hours, I think about how each of my colleagues has her own story of *teshuva* and music; how *Hashem* gathered us from entirely different backgrounds and countries—Russia, France, Colombia, U.S. and Israel—to create a unified sound here in the holy city of Jerusalem. To me, this is no small miracle. And I thank God for it.

Bracha Bdil is an Israeli-British composer, conductor, pianist, and winner of dozens of awards for her compositions, including the Prime Minister's Award for Composition (2022) and the ACUM Award (2019). Her repertoire spans orchestral, chamber, vocal, and electronic music. For concert updates and to join the **Zmora** mailing list:

✉ **zmora@ronshulamit.org.il**
📞 **02-6528531 ext.9**

Chava Rachel Saban studied violin and literature at Yale University, and played with the New Haven Symphony. Her life began anew in Israel where she became a wife, a mother, a grandmother, and a singer of *Tehilim*. She teaches, is a section leader of Zmora and also plays for the elderly.

✉ **havarahel@yahoo.com**

REAL COFFEE TALK WITH SEFIRA

REAL COFFEE TALK WITH SEFIRA

When two powerhouse artists sit down for coffee, the conversation flows as vibrantly as their palettes. In this exclusive interview, Sefira Lightstone—the creative visionary behind Pop Torah, known for her bold, modern, and unapologetic digital expressions of Jewish life—and Dena Ackerman—the fine artist and illustrator whose brush captures faith, femininity, and feeling with exquisite realism—open up about art, light, family, and the beauty of a Jewish woman's creative life.

1. When did you first realize that art was more than a hobby—that it was your calling?

Sefira: Art has always been the way I process life and the world around me. Ever since I was little, you could always find me doodling on school papers or sketching intricate images in my diaries. In high school, I began illustrating for a girls' magazine called *Shoshanim*. I earned about thirty dollars per illustration, which felt like a fortune at the time. I didn't realize then just how deeply I loved drawing, and after high school I stepped away from it for a few years. It wasn't until my mid-twenties, when I was

Sefira Lightstone

2. How do you balance the part of you that wants to experiment freely with the part that knows you need a sustainable practice or brand?

Sefira: The professional side of me knows that building a recognizable brand requires a consistent style. The challenge, especially as an artist, is learning to balance that consistency with creative freedom. I've found that the key is to dig deep and create from your inner voice—to trust the imperfections and let them become part of your signature. It isn't always easy; having a defined style can sometimes feel limiting. But the real sweet spot is when your work flows from that authentic, spiritual place inside you. When you create from there, your art will always feel true, and your brand will naturally follow.

Dena: I haven't balanced it yet. Between client projects, marketing, teaching, raising children, trying to fit in some daily sunshine, exercise, and reading... I feel like there are not enough hours in the day. I often get busy with client work, and

offered a few unexpected illustration jobs, that I finally understood this wasn't just something I enjoyed—it was my passion, and I wanted to pursue it seriously.

Dena: The calling, for me, is seeing something beautiful and needing to recreate it myself. From a young age, I craved ownership over the beauty around me. I saved pictures of beautiful things. I bought books with beautiful illustrations. I copied art that inspired me. I extracted visions from my head and attempted to put them down on paper. I have always felt a need to absorb as much beauty as possible, and share it with others. It gets into your blood. It makes you sacrifice things like sleep and a social life. Like Sefira, it took me a while to recognize it, but I think that feeling was always there.

Dena Ackerman

present, soul and screen.

Dena: I work traditionally, mainly with graphite, colored pencils, ink, watercolor, and acrylic paints. I love being able to create something tangible, imperfections and all.

I have "comfort zone" art... art that comes naturally and easily and helps me earn my bread and butter. Things like pencil drawings, watercolor illustrations, magazine comics. Then there's the "blood, sweat, and tears" art. It comes with the frustration of never being satisfied with what I make, yet I am compelled to continue trying. The struggle to capture the likeness in a portrait. Forcing my acrylic paints to do what I want them to do. Not overworking a watercolor painting. But there's great satisfaction when I come out victorious in the end... it doesn't always happen, but when it does, it makes the fight worthwhile.

4. What's your secret for balancing family, clients, and creativity without losing your joy (or your coffee)?

Sefira: There's definitely coffee involved—but mostly trust in *Hashem*. Some weeks the balance looks effortless, and other weeks it's complete chaos. When times are chaotic, I really call out to Hashem to help me carry through. I've learned to see my family, my faith, and my art as parts of the same story rather than competing priorities. My kids inspire my creativity, my art deepens my connection to *Hashem*, and my work supports the home that anchors it all. When I remember that, even the

then fret about the many, many personal projects I am neglecting. Sometimes I am better at carving out time for them, and sometimes not... but I haven't given up on them. I do not want to die without leaving behind something glorious!

3. What do you each love most about the medium and style you've chosen to work in?

Sefira: For me, digital illustration is where tradition meets modern storytelling. I love that I can take an ancient Hebrew word, a current event, or a moment from *Torah*, and express it with color, texture, and motion that speaks to people scrolling on their phones. It's a bridge—between past and

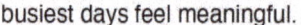

busiest days feel meaningful.

Dena: I love my life and I'm grateful for my many, many blessings. And I drink a lot of tea. I just try my best every day (except for the days when I'm tired of trying and then I get lost in a book or scroll on my phone instead). I think that's all we can do: try our best.

5. What do you wish more people understood about being a Jewish woman artist in today's world?

Sefira: That it's both a privilege and a responsibility. We carry generations of voices within us—women who couldn't always express their stories publicly. So when I create, I feel like I'm giving shape to something larger than myself. It's not about fitting into trends; it's about using beauty to preserve identity, to heal, and to inspire pride in who we are.

Dena: I have a message as an artist, though it doesn't necessarily have to do with being Jewish or female. I'll start by saying that I am humbled and grateful for the support I have gotten from every direction, starting with my parents and grandparents who sent me to art lessons and encouraged me in every way. Teachers and classmates who made a big deal about my doodles. Community members who hired teenage me to create paintings, logos, and illustrations. As an adult, even before I started working as a professional, I received commissions and sold artwork "on the side." And now, as a working artist, I'm overwhelmingly grateful for the support and patronage of people around me, online and off. No artist lives in a vacuum. So this is what I want people to understand: I deeply appreciate you and we artists could not create art without you. Support the artists you love because the world would be a dark place without them.

6. If money, time, and exposure were no barrier, what project would you start tomorrow?

Sefira: I'd build an immersive art experience that tells the story of Jewish resilience—part gallery, part spiritual journey. Visitors could walk through moments of light, exile, and redemption, surrounded by sound, color, and movement. I'd love to paint large-scale pieces by hand in traditional mediums, bringing that tactile, human touch back into the storytelling. It would be a space where ancient stories feel alive again, where every brushstroke carries faith, memory, and hope.

Dena: OMG I'd be like a kid in a candy store... I wouldn't know where to start!!

I've illustrated dozens of books for other people, so a huge dream of mine is to write, illustrate, and publish my own books. I have a number of them in different stages of completion. I want to create picture books, art books, and graphic novels. I want to learn and experiment with new styles of painting and new mediums. I want to travel and create artwork based on the things I see. I have an exciting idea for a series of large paintings that centers around characters from Tanach...

7. Sefira, what's one thing you admire in Dena's process—and Dena, what do you love about Sefira's creative energy?

Sefira: I really admire Dena's watercolor illustrations. She's such an anchor in the Jewish art world—always true to her style and her voice, unwavering, consistent, and deeply positive. Her work has this quiet strength that inspires others to stay authentic. Dena was definitely one of my first inspirations when I was just starting out as an illustrator.

Dena: Wow thank you! That means a lot to me, Sefira. Hands down the thing I love about Sefira's artwork is her passion. You know that whatever she's creating comes from the heart and that there's been a lot of thought and love put into it. When you look at her work, you FEEL things.

8. Sefira, tell us a little bit about the behind-the-scenes process of creating the back cover art piece. What inspired you, and what additional message would you like to share about it?

After searching for a *Chanukah* sweater that truly reflected the holiday, I noticed most designs leaned toward Christian-inspired themes, charming but far from what *Chanukah* stands for. I wanted to create something rooted in Jewish strength and authenticity. The artwork depicts ancient Jerusalem, centered around the original seven-branched Temple *menorah* from the *Beit Hamikdash* where the miracle of light occurred.

This piece is more than festive. It is a declaration of Jewish resilience and connection to our land. *Chanukah* is not about gift-giving or seasonal cheer; it is about holding strong to faith in times of darkness and celebrating the courage to remain who we are. This design carries that message. It is warm and beautiful, but most importantly, it tells the real story of Jewish light and endurance.

ILLUSTRATION BY DENA ACKERMAN

Sefira Lightstone is an Israel-based artist and illustrator whose work bridges Jewish spirituality and modern design. As the lead illustrator for Chabad.org, she has helped shape their visual storytelling with vibrant, meaningful art. Through her platform **@sefiracreative**, she shares illustrations that celebrate faith, resilience, and the beauty of Jewish life.

⊕ sefiracreative.com

Dena Ackerman is a professional artist, illustrator,and art teacher based in Ramat Beit Shemesh. She has illustrated over 40 books and created hundreds of custom paintings for private collectors, businesses, and magazines. Her work is inspired by everyday scenes and emotions, humor, pathos, and the beauty all around us.

⊕ DenaAckerman.com
🅕 🅞 @art_by_Dena

Online art courses:
⊕ artbyDena.thinkific.com

Her Tribe is *Your* Tribe

For you. About you.
Through stories and articles from your sisterhood – women who uplift, inspire, and celebrate Jewish life *together.*

If you're enjoying this magazine – what's the next step?

Subscribe to our upcoming editions –
Purim • Pesach • Shavuot • Summer

Have a meaningful story to share?
We'd love to hear it!
Reach out to submit your article or idea.

Want your AD featured next time?
Promote your brand to thousands of Jewish women worldwide and support a growing project built with heart and purpose.

Sponsors & Partners & Investors Welcome!
Help us reach new locations, grow our team, expand our reach, and keep this magazine shining.
Your support makes the difference.

🌐 tinyurl.com/Hertribemag
✉️ hello@hertribemagazine.com
📷 f ▶️ @hertribemagazine

HER TRIBE

Chanukah Classics, the Sephardic Way—

Crisp, Bright, and Beautifully Jewish

Chanukah is known for its delicious foods and for bringing people together.

Best friends Shana and Dikla believe the best celebrations happen around a table filled with variety—dishes that honor tradition, nourish the body, and celebrate loved ones. That's why they've mixed lighter favorites from Shana's kitchen with family classics inspired by their grandmothers—one Moroccan, one Tunisian. Most of the recipes are vegan, all are vegetarian, and each one is simply delicious!

Tunisian Banatage (Potato Fritters)—
Shana's Grandmother
Mathilda Mimun's Recipe

As a child, I always begged my grandmother to make these for me any time of the year. These golden fritters are a fun alternative to *latkes*—crisp on the outside, soft and comforting inside, with a touch of Middle Eastern warmth. Delicious plain or with dips and salads.

Ingredients:

2 cups mashed potatoes (not too moist)

2 eggs, well beaten

¼ cup cake meal or matzah meal

Salt and pepper, to taste

Optional: a sprinkle of cinnamon or paprika

½ cup matzah meal or flour, for coating

½ cup vegetable oil (for frying)

Instructions:

In a medium bowl, combine mashed potatoes, beaten eggs, cake meal, salt, pepper, and optional spices.

Mix until the texture is soft but holds its shape. Adjust with a bit more cake meal or a touch of water if needed.

Shape mixture into small patties, about 2-3 inches in diameter.

Lightly coat each patty in *matzah* meal or flour, shaking off excess.

Heat vegetable oil in a skillet over medium heat (enough to cover the bottom, about ¼ inch).

Fry patties in batches, 2–3 minutes per side, until golden brown and crisp.

Remove from the pan and drain on paper towels. Serve warm.

Honeyness Honey Mustard Kale Salad with Oranges and Cashews

BY SHANA BALKIN, SALAD THERAPY

Sweet, tart, and savory—the perfect fresh counterbalance to the richness of traditional fried faves.

Ingredients:

Honeyless Honey Mustard Vegan Dressing:

⅓ cup Vegan Sunflower Seed Sour Cream (or other unsweetened, unflavored vegan sour cream or yogurt)

1½ tablespoons yellow mustard

1½ tablespoons coconut aminos

Pinch of black pepper

Salad:

5 oz chopped kale- about 6 1/2 loosely packed cups

⅓ c dry roasted unsalted cashews

¼ pomegranate arils (optional)

¼ medium onion- ½ cup slices, loosely packed

4 clementine oranges

Method:

Peel and segment your clementine oranges, slice your onion to your taste, and give a rough chop to your cashews.

Toss thoroughly and enjoy!

Cilantro Pesto

BY SHANA BALKIN, SALAD THERAPY

A zesty, green, oil-free sauce full of freshness and versatility—amazing with broka, *X*, or roasted vegetables for a burst of flavor.

Ingredients:

4 ounces fresh cilantro

Juice of 1 lemon

½ heaping cup raw cashews

1 large clove garlic

¾ teaspoons salt

Method:

Blend all ingredients in the food processor for about one minute, scraping down the sides of the bowl periodically as needed to ensure even blending.

When the pesto is done, you should have a puree that's pretty homogenous but still has some texture.

Serve and enjoy!

Moroccan Sfinge (Dikla's Family Recipe)

Light, airy Moroccan doughnuts traditionally fried in oil and dipped in sugar—a *Chanukah* classic that connects generations. This sfinge recipe was passed down from Dikla's grandmother Sultana z"l. Dikla's son is named in her honor.

Ingredients:

1 Tbsp dry yeast

1½ cups warm water

3 cups flour

½ tsp salt

Oil for frying

Sugar for dusting

Instructions:

In a large bowl, dissolve yeast in warm water and let it bubble for 10–15 minutes.

Add flour and salt; mix well until sticky but smooth. Let rise, covered, for 1–2 hours, until doubled.

With oiled hands, pull small portions of dough, shape into rings, and carefully drop into hot oil.

Fry until golden on both sides. Drain and roll in sugar.

Best eaten warm, straight from the pan.

Shana Balkin is the creator of saladtherapy.com and is co-founder of MindBody Judaism. Drawing on Chassidus and modern science, she helps women embody Jewish teachings, using their bodies and the physical world around them as vessels to channel G-dliness, fulfillment, and purpose into everyday life. She lives in Houston, Texas, with her husband and three children.

@mindbodyjudaism

Dikla Pickelner is an educator, co-founder of MindBody Judaism, and owner of MNB Clinic. She guides women through personal and spiritual transformation, helping them challenge distorted beliefs and clear the inner channels that block Divine flow—opening the way to hear, trust, and live from their own G-dly wisdom. Dikla lives with her husband and children in Houston, Texas.

@mindbodyjudaism

Chanukah in Israel is one of my favorite holidays. It feels like a full season of light, color, and creativity— from glowing *chanukiot* to endless trays of donuts in every bakery. It's also a time to get playful in the kitchen and try something new. These two recipes are a taste of that spirit— festive, flavorful, and made to share. Enjoy!

Savory Sufganiyot with Feta & Za'atar

Makes: About 15 medium sufganiyot

Ingredients

For the dough:

3 ½ cups (450 g) all-purpose flour

2 ¼ tsp (1 packet) instant yeast

3 Tbsp sugar

1 tsp salt

1 cup (240 ml) warm milk (or water for pareve)

2 eggs

3 Tbsp olive oil

For frying:

Neutral oil (canola, sunflower, or peanut), enough for 2–3 inches depth

For the filling:

200 g (7 oz) feta cheese, crumbled

½ cup cream cheese or labneh

1 Tbsp olive oil

1 clove garlic, finely grated

2 Tbsp chopped fresh parsley or dill

Black pepper, to taste

For topping:

2 Tbsp olive oil

1 Tbsp za'atar spice blend

Flaky salt (optional)

Instructions

1. Make the dough

In a large bowl, whisk together flour, yeast, sugar, and salt.

Add warm milk, eggs, and olive oil. Mix until a dough forms.

Knead on a floured surface (or in a stand mixer with a dough hook) until smooth and elastic, about 8-10 minutes.

Place in an oiled bowl, cover, and let rise 1-1½ hours, until doubled in size.

2. Shape and fry

Roll dough to ½ inch thick. Cut circles with a 2½–3 inch cutter.

Place on parchment, cover lightly, and let rise again for 30–40 minutes.

Heat oil to 170–175°C (340–350°F). Fry *sufganiyot* in batches for about 1-2 minutes per side, until golden.

Drain on paper towels.

3. Make the filling

Blend feta, cream cheese or labneh, olive oil, garlic, and herbs until smooth and creamy.
If too thick, add a splash of milk or water. Season with black pepper.

4. Fill the *sufganiyot*

Once cool enough to handle, poke a hole in each donut with a skewer or piping tip.
Pipe in the feta filling generously.

5. Finish and serve

Brush tops with olive oil.
Sprinkle with za'atar and flaky salt.

Gelt Lava Cakes

Ingredients

For the molten centers:

8 chocolate gelt coins (use good-quality dark or milk chocolate)

2 Tbsp heavy cream (or coconut cream for dairy-free)

For the cake batter:

170 g (6 oz) good-quality dark chocolate (60–70%)

115 g (½ cup) unsalted butter (or margarine for dairy-free)

2 whole eggs + 2 egg yolks

½ cup (100 g) sugar

¼ cup (30 g) flour

Pinch of salt

For finishing:

Gold dust or luster powder (optional, for "gelt shine")

Powdered sugar, for dusting

Instructions

1. Make the molten centers

Melt the gelt coins with 2 Tbsp cream over low heat until smooth.

Pour into a silicone mini ice cube tray (or line a small tray and freeze flat).

Freeze until solid (at least 1 hour). You'll get about 6 frozen chocolate "coin" inserts.

2. Make the batter

Melt chocolate and butter together (microwave in 20-second bursts or use a double boiler).

In a separate bowl, whisk eggs, yolks, and sugar until thick and pale (about 2 minutes).

Fold in the melted chocolate mixture.

Sift in flour and salt, then fold until just combined.

3. Assemble the cakes

Grease and flour 6 ramekins (or muffin tins).

Fill each about two-thirds full with batter.

Place one frozen "coin" insert in the center, pressing lightly.

Cover with a spoonful of more batter so it's hidden.

4. Bake

Bake at 220°C (425°F) for 11–13 minutes—edges should be set and centers slightly jiggly.

Let rest for 1 minute, then carefully invert onto plates.

5. Finish & serve

Dust with powdered sugar.

Lightly brush with edible gold dust to mimic real gelt.

Talia Krief is a social media manager by trade and a foodie at heart. She specializes in creating social strategies and authentic content that help brands connect with their audiences in a real, relatable way. Beyond managing accounts and building communities, Talia brings her passion for food to life through recipe development and creative collaborations with culinary brands.

@krief_kitchen
bitesizedmedia.co

THE POWER OF SISTERHOOD:
The ASHIRA Story

BY SHOSHANNA STEIN BENARROCH

I first came across Ashira Boutique at a vibrant community bazaar in Bal Harbour, FL. What caught my attention were the clothes, but I stayed for the mission. There was a buzz around their corner of the event, a little pocket of light drawing people in. Women were smiling, trying on pieces, talking with one another. The energy was radiant and spiritual, the kind of joy that you can feel before you even understand where it's coming from.

When I met founder Esther Toledano soon after, I became emotional. As she began sharing her vision, I felt something stir deep inside because at one point in my life, I also needed a sisterhood and it didn't exist. I had longed for a space where women could hold one another up, a place that would empower and strengthen us when we needed it most. What struck me most was her quiet strength and unwavering belief that "empowered women change homes, and empowered homes change communities." Her vision began during a deeply personal turning point in her life. She explained, "I wanted to create a place where women could come exactly as they are, feel safe, and find their strength again."

Esther Toledano and Tanya Altit at a *Hafrashat Challah* for *Rachel Imeinu*.

Ashira Jewish Women Center and Ashira Boutique grew from that seed. They were built to meet both the heart and the day-to-day needs of women, offering connection, dignity, and opportunity in one space. "This isn't just a boutique," Esther said. "It's a

movement of women helping women build their lives back up."

Ashira's programs reflect that mission in action. The Boutique provides dignified, flexible employment and skills training. Women learn retail operations, customer care, and merchandising while working in a supportive, uplifting environment. "It's about giving women more than a job," Esther shared. "It's about giving them back their confidence."

"Business Women Networking" connects entrepreneurs and professionals to help them grow, thrive, and support one another's success from within the community. "*Hatzalah* for the *Neshama*" offers emotional support and guidance to women in crisis, giving them a space to be heard and held. Daily Classes and Workshops create an atmosphere of

Participants in a monthly *Rosh Chodesh* event

Women's Inspiring event with guest speaker Charlene Aminoff, (second from the left)

became part of the community, volunteering and showing up for others, rediscovering her own strength. Her transformation, from isolation to empowerment, reflects what happens every day at Ashira.

Community is at the core of it all. Volunteers greet, organize, teach, restock, call, deliver, and simply sit beside other women who need someone there. "This is a place where you don't have to prove anything," Esther said. "You just have to show up. We'll meet you there." That simple culture of presence and sisterhood turns individual healing into collective strength.

Ashira's sustainability model mirrors its mission. The Boutique is not a side project; it's part of the heartbeat of the organization. Sales, partnerships, and training feed directly into the center's programs, helping them grow and reach more women. "We built it with heart, but also with strategy," Esther explained. "Purpose needs a plan, and the plan needs people."

shared learning and sisterhood, ranging from spiritual growth to practical skills. "We meet women where they are," she explained. "And we remind them they don't have to walk alone."

One story that captures this spirit began with a woman who came to the boutique during a difficult chapter in her life. She wasn't sure what she was looking for other than a sense of belonging. She was welcomed without judgment, offered space to breathe, learn, and be held. Over time she

Ashira's impact as a sisterhood is clear. The programs have steadily expanded, more women are being supported, and the sense of community continues to grow. "Every time a woman walks in and finds her footing again, that's a milestone for us," she said.

Looking ahead, Esther sees a future where Ashira's doors open even wider. "I want more women to feel what it's like to walk into a place that already believes in them," she said. She dreams of expanding workshops, creating more job opportunities, and inspiring similar spaces around the world. Her message to women everywhere is simple: "You are not alone. You are needed. Your next step is welcome here."

Ashira and Her Tribe Magazine are just two examples of the quiet power that's created when women come together with love, compassion, and shared purpose. When we lift one another with open hearts, we create light that reaches far beyond ourselves. Sisterhood has always been at the heart and strength of *Am Yisrael*. It is how we hold one another up, how we create safety, how we keep our people strong. When one sisterhood reaches out to another, it forms a powerful, unbreakable net of *chesed*, support, and love. Through this web of connection, we build the grassroots strength to create real change for our people.

This is an invitation to join that light. Follow their journey, support their work, and become part of this growing movement. And if your heart is calling you to do so, bring this sisterhood to your own community. Together, we can weave a network of strength that transforms lives and uplifts *Am Yisrael*.

Esther Toledano is the founder of Ashira Jewish Women Center and Ashira Boutique in North Miami. She leads a mission that blends empowerment, community, and practical support for women through workshops, crisis guidance, networking, and dignified employment. Esther believes that empowered women build healthy homes and vibrant communities, and she works every day to make that vision real.

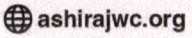
ashirajwc.org

Shoshanna Stein Benarroch is a teacher, artist, and mentor whose *chizuk* radiates from a deep awareness of *Hashem's* love. Founder of the Ki Tov Project, she inspires others to seek divine goodness in every moment and see *Hashem* everywhere.

Find her:
 @MySoCalledJewishLife

One Heart, One Nation

A LEADERSHIP Q&A
WITH CHERIE ALBUCHER

INTERVIEW BY NAOMI JOURNO | HER TRIBE MAGAZINE

hen Cherie Albucher made *aliyah* at sixteen, she never imagined how deeply she'd shape communities, businesses, and women's leadership in Israel. From her IDF service to producing luxury events, leading *aliyah* initiatives, and founding women's empowerment forums, her journey is one of faith, resilience, and vision. In this open and heartfelt conversation, Cherie shares how she defines success, finds light through challenge, and why leadership sometimes starts with red lipstick.

How did you step into leadership, and what makes your approach unique?

Cherie: I made *aliyah* at sixteen, studied in the first Naale program for English speakers, and later joined the army. Serving in the medical corps during the Intifada was my first true leadership experience, it showed me what it means to serve with purpose and I knew from that point onwards my mission was to serve and do something incredible for this country.

After the army, I worked for an Israeli business magnate who specialized in reviving struggling companies. Managing projects across real estate, energy, and construction taught me how to build strategy, lead teams, think out of the box and create results. Later, I joined the international jewelry brand H. Stern marketing team, producing product launches, events, learning the art of branding, storytelling, PR and advertising.

But my true calling came in 2006, when I had the opportunity to work as the Modi'in's *Aliyah* Coordinator, running a special *aliyah* program in conjunction with the Ministry of Absorption, the Jewish Agency and the Modi'in municipality. I helped over 750 families make *aliyah* and integrate into Israeli life. After 9 years in the position, I realized *aliyah* doesn't end with arrival—people need emotional, social, and financial tools to thrive. In 2015, I opened my own business, combining my marketing, strategy, and community building to help *olim* and small businesses grow. My approach blends Israeli boldness with Anglo structure and empathy—strategy with soul.

How do you personally define success in leadership and in life?

Cherie: Success isn't about money. It's when a client calls because they heard, "You need to work with Cherie," or when voters trust me to represent them on city council. But the truest success is personal.

It's sitting at my *Rosh Hashanah* table surrounded by family after a hard two years and realizing we're still standing. It's watching my oldest daughter build a home with her husband, to watch my second daughter serve in the army with courage, my third daughter face anxiety with strength, and my little boy dream big. Those are my victories. Leadership begins at home.

What's your approach to partnerships, and how do you navigate differences?

Cherie: Collaboration starts with self-awareness. You are your brand—walk into every room confident yet open-minded. Listen before you speak and ask yourself, *How can I grow from this?*

During Corona, I launched the *Support Small Businesses* platform, bringing together twelve experts to offer daily guidance to 350 Anglo business owners. We weren't competitors—we were a community. That's how I see leadership: creating connection, not competing.

When collaborations end, do it with grace. Everyone has an ego, but dignity lasts longer than disagreement. Always be the person others speak well of when you're not in the room.

A highlight of my journey has been

The *Shabbat* Project in Modi'in

working with IWEN—the Israeli Women Entrepreneurs Network. Together we produced leadership programs and retreats that celebrate women who lead with purpose. IWEN embodies women supporting women, building something larger than ourselves.

Where does your passion come from?

Cherie: Jewish women are born leaders. The *Torah* gives us tools to build and to nurture. I wanted to create spaces that help women express that strength. That's how the Women's Empowerment Meetups began—giving women a stage to share, grow, and support one another.

I remember one session that began with a single word—*feminism*. The discussion that followed was fiery, honest, and inspiring. It reminded me that leadership looks different for every woman, and that's the beauty of it.

My grandmother always said, "No matter how you feel, put on your red lipstick." For her, that small act symbolized strength, not vanity. It became my signature reminder: confidence is a choice. Some days leadership is heels and lipstick; other days it's flip-flops and baby food stains. Both are beautiful, both are real.

What advice would you give to women stepping into leadership?

Cherie: Start where you are. Don't wait for perfection. Leadership grows one step at a time.

For women already leading—pause and ask if your goals still align with your purpose. Leadership isn't about saying yes to everything; sometimes it's about saying no. The bravest act a leader can take is to rest and realign.

Tell us about your work with the Shabbat Project and how it reflects your leadership.

Cherie: The *Shabbat* Project is one of my proudest achievements. After seeing thousands of women in South Africa close the streets for a massive *challah* bake, I thought, "We need that in Israel."

When I brought it to Modi'in, it quickly became a phenomenon—each year, bigger, brighter, and more joyful. Even during Corona, my partners and I held a virtual *challah* bake with 300 women. And during the war, when people said, "How can you do this now?" I answered, *If not now, when?*

We had no budget, but 300 women still showed up to dance, cry, and celebrate unity. That's Jewish leadership—creating light in the dark. The *Shabbat* Project isn't about religion; it's about belonging. Every Jewish woman can find herself in *Shabbat. One Heart, One Nation*

How do you deal with burnout, procrastination, and imposter syndrome?

Cherie:
BURNOUT: When the war began, my business paused. My daughter entered the army, and I felt completely drained. I told a colleague, "I can't lead right now." She replied, "That is leadership." That moment changed me. Recognizing your limits is strength. Rest, heal, then rebuild.

PROCRASTINATION: We all face it. I constantly ask myself, *Is this good enough? Should I wait?* But I've learned to act, even imperfectly. Mistakes are part of growth—progress matters more than perfection.

IMPOSTER SYNDROME: Every woman feels it. There's always someone who seems more confident or accomplished. But *Hashem* made each of us unique for a reason. I remind myself—I'm not trying to be anyone else, just the best version of me. And that's enough.

What did Corona and the war teach you about leadership?

Cherie: Corona taught me creativity and the power of community. The war taught me humility and faith. It broke me but rebuilt me stronger. I learned that leadership isn't about being on stage— it's about showing up for others, even when you're on your knees.

True leadership can be quiet. It's the mother praying for her children, the friend who checks in, the business owner who keeps going despite everything. It's found in the details, in the doing, in the heart.

What message would you like to share for Hanukkah?

Cherie: I've been privileged to work with *Or LaMishpachot – Light for Families*, an organization supporting bereaved families who lost loved ones in the war. That's what light really means—helping others find the light in the dark.

Hanukkah isn't just eight nights; it's a way of life. Every act of kindness, faith, or strength passes the flame forward. The *menorah* teaches us that light grows when shared. You are the candle, you are the light and the people around you are your *menorah*. Together, we shine brighter.

Cherie Lipschitz Albucher
Originally from South Africa, Cherie Albucher brings over two decades of experience in project management, marketing, and corporate events. A councilwoman in Modi'in–Maccabim–Reut, certified director, and active board member, she's recognized for empowering Jewish women through leadership initiatives, conferences, and community programs that unite business, faith, and personal growth.

From Passion to Profit:

Why authenticity is still the most powerful marketing strategy ▶▶▶

BY ABBEY WOLIN

When people ask how I turned my passion into a business, I usually smile and say, "By noticing the gaps."

I've always been obsessed with what's missing—the holes in the market, the untapped needs, the spaces that quietly beg to be filled. My first gap was simple: I loved art, but there weren't many hand-painted Judaica pieces around. So I started painting.

I tried wood, then paper, and finally glass. One Sunday I set up a small table at a street fair. By the end of the day, every piece was gone. That's when it hit me: maybe this hobby wasn't just a hobby.

Of course, realizing that and building a business are two different things. When a boutique owner asked if I'd considered wholesaling, I didn't even know what that meant. The idea sounded great until I ran the numbers— my profit disappeared. That lesson taught me something I repeat to every woman I mentor: enthusiasm is wonderful, but math is non-negotiable. You can't price by feeling; you price by reality—time, materials, and value.

Back then, there wasn't much business education for Orthodox women. I asked for help, but no one could really guide me. I had to learn the long way— through trial, error, and persistence. That experience shaped my mission today: to be the woman I needed when I was starting out. I never want another woman to feel alone at the starting line.

JUST START— EVEN IF IT'S AWKWARD

When I tell women to begin, they often whisper, "But I'm not ready." Neither was I. I've shown up online with braces, swollen from medication, bad lighting, messy hair—and still pressed "post." Because your voice is sacred. If you silence it out of fear, you might be withholding the very message Hashem wants you to share. Perfection isn't holy; courage is.

The market will tell you what works— just like social media. You don't make something go viral; the people do. The same is true for business. The key is to listen, learn, and adjust. Failure isn't a stop sign; it's part of the process. What separates successful entrepreneurs from the rest is how quickly they get up, brush themselves off, and keep going. Grit—both physical and emotional—is what builds a lasting business.

WHAT "AUTHENTIC ENGAGEMENT" REALLY MEANS

Authenticity online isn't about filters or trends; it's about showing up as yourself. Your feed is your storefront, but your stories and DMs are where real connection happens. Ask questions. Use polls. Talk to your followers as if they're friends sitting across your kitchen table. Tell stories that make them laugh, cry, or nod in recognition.

One of my simplest posts—Six Things Every Jewish Woman Can Do to Bring Blessing into Her Life—went viral. It wasn't flashy; it was honest and rooted in Torah values. That's what people respond to: truth that feels personal.

If you're juggling multiple channels, schedule time for engagement. I check messages in the morning and evening; that's plenty. Consistency matters more than constant activity. And if your inbox is overflowing, there are tools that can pull comments from every platform into one dashboard—but the heart of engagement can't be automated. Keep your voice in it.

Remember: it's not about you, it's about them. Every caption, story, or post should make your audience feel seen, inspired, or understood. When you create from that place, you build trust—and trust converts.

Authenticity doesn't mean overexposure. I love to dance, but I don't dance on camera. I won't film in pajamas or robes, not because I'm hiding, but because boundaries keep me aligned with the message I want to send. Authenticity is intentional, not impulsive.

And if you hate being on camera? Don't. Many successful creators never show their faces. Film your hands, your process, your environment—or pair meaningful footage with text and voiceovers. Connection is about substance, not selfies.

COMMUNICATE GENEROUSLY

Some women worry about "spamming" their followers. I promise, most of us under-communicate. Post often, but with purpose. Stories are your conversation; your feed is your legacy. Choose one or two platforms that feel natural—go deep there, not wide everywhere.

SCALING WITH SANITY

Growth is exciting—and dangerous if you chase it blindly. Before expanding, I always ask three questions:

1. Do I have the cash to support this move?

2. Do I have the people and systems to manage it?

3. Does my gut feel calm and open about it?

Numbers matter, but intuition matters too. If something looks profitable but feels constricting, I don't do it. When something fills me with calm determination, I take the leap. I've learned that your body often knows before your brain does.

Sometimes growth means bootstrapping—reinvesting profits instead of taking them out. Sometimes it means saying no to something shiny that doesn't fit your season. Sustainable success is quieter than hustle culture admits. Expansion should serve your life, not consume it.

TURNING ENGAGEMENT INTO INCOME

Marketing is about relationship, not quick returns. I use what I call the "jab, jab, jab, hook" method: give value, give again, give again, then ask. Teach, inspire, entertain—and then invite your audience to take the next step. People appreciate direction when they already trust you.

You can't expect to put in $100 and get $100 back tomorrow. Marketing is long-term, like compound interest. Every post, ad, and story adds another layer of recognition. Over time, people buy because they already know and trust you.

When evaluating marketing ROI (Return on investment), look beyond money. There's emotional ROI too—energy, joy, peace of mind. If a project makes financial sense but drains your spirit, the real return is negative. If it lights you up and aligns with your values, it's worth the investment.

PROTECT YOUR ENERGY

I've burned out more times than I can count. Now I plan recovery the way I plan campaigns. Every week I get a manicure—my personal act of self-respect. I work outdoors whenever possible; the sound of water near my home resets me instantly.

If you don't rest, you'll crack. Taking time for yourself isn't indulgent; it's strategic. A woman's energy is her business capital. Your company can only grow as sustainably as you do.

MY FINAL ADVICE

Start messy. Price bravely. Serve genuinely. Rest deliberately.

You will fail, and that's part of the curriculum. Success belongs to the ones who keep rising—with faith, humility, and grit.

Your passion is not random; it's your assignment. Trust that Hashem gave it to you for a reason, and build something that brings light to others while keeping your own flame burning bright.

Abbey Wolin is a business strategist and founder of a marketing agency that helps entrepreneurs and organizations discover their market gaps, build authentic engagement, and scale sustainably. She is passionate about empowering Jewish women to create businesses that align with purpose, faith, and joy.

 @abbeywolin